ONLINE SAFETY

SCAMS, SPAM, VIRUSES AND CLOUDS

A. M. PERRY

Table of Contents

Foreword

This guide is a continual work in progress. Its audience is primarily those who are unfamiliar with computers and technology and are worried about the security of their computer or being the subject of a scam or fraud. However, even those familiar with computers may benefit from the following collection of ideas and anecdotes.

The world of computers and technology constantly changes. As it changes, so does the criminal aspect; those looking to extort money and cause chaos. As one problem is fixed, another arises.

The idea for this guide came about following discussions with my local Neighbourhood Watch community. I realised that staying safe online was as important these days as locking your door, or reporting suspicious activity down your street. If we keep a watch out for each other in our actual communities, we should do the same for our online communities.

As in real life, those most vulnerable are those most targeted. Unfortunately, there will always be someone out there looking to exploit and manipulate others for their own self-interest. I doubt we'll ever stop this, but we can make things harder for them.

That is the aim of this guide. Its intention is to provide simple steps on protecting yourself from scams, fraud and crime within the online world. The guide has been put together based on my own experiences, with input from friends, family and the online and local community. Even though I've worked in IT for twenty years and played around on computers for even longer, I've almost fallen for scams and even ended up with a virus trying to extort money from me. It can happen to anyone, so don't be scared or embarrassed if it happens to you. Learn from your experience and share it with others so they won't experience the same. Just as important: don't let an unpleasant experience put you off from using your computer, or embracing the amazing ways we can connect with one another using the Internet.

I've asked the local community and the online world for ideas on the best way to prevent scams, fraud and viruses. I've asked about the subjects that most concern people, and for general advice on staying safe online. The response has been amazing, and credit goes to everyone who has asked questions, provided ideas and feedback into this guide.

There is no silver bullet to staying completely safe in the online world, but you can exercise care and that all important gut-feeling that something might be wrong. This guide will give you enough information to question whether something is right, and how to react if you have concerns about staying safe online.

How the guide works (and will grow)

What follows is a set of ideas and pointers for protecting yourself and your computer equipment (laptop, tablet, phone, etc.) from scams, viruses and unwanted nasties.

I've broken the sections into primary headings and sub-sections of basics, intermediate and advanced. Each section will have a key lesson. If you take anything away from this guide, let it be the key lessons. The intermediate and advanced sections may be useful, but if you are unfamiliar with computers, they may be more of a hinderance than a help.

At the end of the guide, there is a list of ideas for the next version. My intention is to update the guide with new information based on continual feedback. This is because new ideas are being generated all the time and if I waited for them all, the guide would never be complete. It also gives the reader a taster of what to expect or to provide their own thoughts on what they'd like to see in the next version.

This is not intended to be my view of the world of online security, but a joint effort for everyone. It's only a start and your input into this guide will be key as we share ideas to help one another.

If there's anything in this guide you'd like to see, that you disagree with, or think can be improved upon, please contact me via:

www.cybersecuritycommunity.co.uk

Running your own Cyber Security Community Workshop

This guide has now been used on a number of occasions to run Cyber Security evenings with my neighbours.

If you're interested in running your own workshop to help local communities with Cyber Security related issues, then I'd love to hear from you and help where I can. Please contact me at either of my websites.

Disclaimer

No advice is 100% guaranteed. Indeed, there is no 100% way of avoiding scams, viruses or having your computer hacked, the same way no amount of alarms, CCTV or security guards will ever 100% stop a burglary. If someone wants to hack you or steal your details, they'll find a way - your job is to make it as hard for them as possible.

Security in IT is the same in real life; it is about slowing down the intruder and making them think twice about whether their attack is worth pursuing. The same way we add locks on our doors, install alarms in our house and even these days, install CCTV; applying good practice to our online security will deter someone trying to access your computer.

Generally, most hacks or scams are the circumstance of mistakes, or what's known in the industry as 'human error'. We forget to change our password, we unlock our phone in full view of a crowded train, or announce our credit card and address details to the office when making a purchase over the phone. We're all human and we all make mistakes, as you'll see later in this guide.

Following the advice throughout this guide will help you avoid scams, hacks or computer security issues, but it won't guarantee it will never happen. There are lots of reasons for this, one of the main being that new viruses, hacking attempts, computer software issues, etc. are always appearing on the horizon, ready to be exploited by criminals, scammers and hackers.

What this guide does offer is some common-sense advice on how to be aware of the people who perform these scams and hacks, their methods and how to protect yourself. I hope it will help, and I hope you stay safe online (and in real life).

The legal bit

Although the author and publisher have made every effort to ensure that the information in this book was correct at time of press, the author and publisher do not assume and hereby disclaim any liability to any party for any loss, damage, or disruption caused by errors or omissions, whether such errors or omissions result from negligence, accident, or any other cause.

Credits and Acknowledgements

The following people have been fantastic in providing support and proof-reading skills (in either the English language or technical aspects - or both), and have helped make the guide what it is today.

Shirley and David Rollitt

Rebecca Travers

Debbie Travers

Darrell Strike

Neil Boyle

Martin Sharp

Pam & Haz Furness

Janet Perry

John Bradley

The LinkedIn Community

The Neighbourhood Watch Community

About the Author

I'm sure you're itching to get reading, so I'll keep this bit brief.

I've worked in IT for as long as I can remember, and messed around with computers for even longer. I've always had an interest for new technology, even at the age of three when I showed my Mum how to use our new VHS video player. I'm fortunate that it's led me into a very interesting career. I've worked across a variety of sectors, including financial, aviation and pharmaceutical, performing roles from helpdesk support to running multi-million pound projects.

Because computers and technology is my hobby, I also find myself helping family and friends fix and secure their computers, tablets or mobile phones. Much of the advice in this guide is precisely what I give when I'm helping people out.

As well as a career in IT, I'm also embarking on a career as a writer. My aim is to write fiction and poetry and hopefully, one day, find an audience who will read it. Writing a book on computer and online safety seemed a good bridge from one career to the other, as well as good practice.

I hope you enjoy it. More information on this guide and some of my other projects can be found on my website:

www.andrewmarkperry.com

Glossary

Glossaries are generally alphabetical. However, the following compilation of terms, synonyms and definitions are presented in an order that guides you through the terminology. For example, it is better we first understand what a *Virus* is, before we consider *Adware*.

Term	Also known as	Description
Device	Hardware, Computer, tablet, mobile phone, machine	A device is the computer, tablet, mobile phone, etc. you are using to connect to the Internet. For the purposes of this guide, the term 'device' will be used consistently to refer to any of the possibilities.
Internet	Cloud, Web, Website, Information Superhighway (a horrible term used by the media years ago)	When you connect your device to the Internet, you become part of a larger mesh of computers. All these computers can communicate with one another using various means, e.g. web pages, emails, chat programs.
Cloud	Internet	The Cloud **is** the Internet.
Online	Connected, Web	Connecting your computer, tablet or mobile phone device to the Internet
Internet Provider	ISP	Effectively, the utility company that provides your Internet service, like another utility company would provide your water or electric.
Data	Information, files, documents	Data is what is produced by you or someone else on a computer. It can be anything from a word-processor document, a picture or emails.
Scam	Social engineering	When someone, either by phone, email or message, tries to extort money or something from you by illegitimate means.

Term	Also known as	Description
Firewall	Router (although not technically the same thing), Wi-Fi box, Windows Firewall	A firewall is a computer program or device that protects unwanted people from accessing your computer from the Internet. Most modern routers that your Internet Provider supplies have a firewall built in. Also, modern Windows and Mac machines have a firewall built in to protect you when connecting to public WiFi hotspots.
Router	Wi-Fi box	A router is a device that bridges the connection between your devices and your Internet Provider. It takes the connections from your devices (often using Wi-Fi) and *routes* them to the Internet.
Wi-Fi	Network, Wireless, Local Area Network, hotspot	Wi-Fi is a radio signal that devices use to connect to each other and the Internet without cables.
Software	Application, App, Programme, Services	Something you run on your device, such as a chat programme, or a word processor. Software runs on Hardware.
Operating system	OS, Windows, MacOS, Android, iOS, Linux	A particular type of software that runs on your device, and allows other software to run. Without an Operating System, your device wouldn't be able to do anything. Typically this is the first software that runs when you switch on your PC, Mac or mobile phone.
Reboot	Restart, Bounce	What IT people make a career out of telling people to do – the secret is: it works! Rebooting your computer is the act of shutting it down and starting it up again. A bit like you switch the ignition to your car off, and switch it back on again. Rebooting a computer can sometimes clean up any software issues that you might be experiencing. If the issue still appears after a reboot, then it's time to investigate some more.

Term	Also known as	Description
Service	SaaS, Cloud, software, Online Service	A service online may be something like your online banking, or grocery shopping. It may even be where you upload your photographs to. A service is effectively Software on the Internet.
Patches	Patching, Updates, fixes, bug fixes	Patches are updates to your computer software that provide increased security and new features. Consider a patch like an inoculation – it is optional, but highly recommended to protect you and your computer from viruses
Virus	Malware, Trojan	An unwanted, and likely harmful piece of software that you do not want on your device.
Adware	Virus, malware, trojan, ransomware	Like a virus, but intended to plague you with Adverts and pop-ups until your computer slows to a halt.
Anti-virus	AV, Anti-malware	Computer software designed to detect and stop viruses and Adware on your computer. Anti-virus software is fallible, so don't 100% rely on it.
Email	Electronic Mail	A method of communicating with one another and organisations on the Internet by sending electronic messages. Emails can be intercepted, so be careful about what information you send in them.
Attachments	Email Attachments	It is possible to send a picture, or document file in an email – these are known as attachments. Generally, attachments from people you trust are OK. If you receive an attachment from someone you don't recognise, then raise your suspicion levels immediately.
SPAM	Unsolicited email	Email you didn't ask for and do not want. SPAM can lead to nastier problems like viruses or phishing.

Term	Also known as	Description
Hacked	Compromised, attacked, breached	When someone accesses your device, or online service, e.g. email, without your consent. This might be because they've guessed your password and been able to log into your account.
Phishing	SPAM, virus	Phishing is a means of tricking you into accessing a website or service that is fraudulent. For example, a Phishing email may be an email pretending to be from your bank, that directs you to a website that looks to be your bank, when in fact it is fake and is trying to steal your password or confidential details such as bank account numbers, etc.
Password	PIN code, Secret	A serious of letters and/or numbers that allow you to log into software or services
Browser	Web Browser, Internet Explorer, Chrome, Safari, Firefox, Opera	A piece of software used to view web pages and access services on the web, such as your email, or photographs.
Search Engine	Google, Bing	A method of finding websites or services on the Internet without knowing the website's address. A bit like a searchable telephone directory with links.
Link	Hyperlink, shortcut, URL, Internet Favourite	Links appear on websites and emails and are ways of quickly directing you to web pages or online services.
Certificate	Padlock, Website Security, https, encrypted, SSL	A web site with a certificate is one you generally trust and has proved they are who they say they are. A certificate will also encrypt your data, which means no one will be able to see what you're uploading or downloading.

Term	Also known as	Description
Upload / Download	Send, pull, stream, receive	Uploading is the act of sending your data, such as pictures, personal details, etc. to the Internet. Downloading is the act of retrieving data, such as movies, pictures, etc. from the Internet. Streaming a movie is a form of downloading.
Social media	Online Presence	Online Computer software where you can upload pictures of your dinner, or tell the world you're going on holiday. Something that's not recommended without looking at your privacy settings.
Privacy Settings	Public Sharing	Ability to tailor who can and can't see your social media posts. Be careful: some social media services automatically set a public option, meaning anyone can see your posts.
Multi-factor Authentication	MFA, Two-factor authentication, dongle, smart card, token	A way of improving the security of your online services by combining your password or pin, with your mobile phone or another device. The idea is that anyone trying to steal your details will not have both your password/pin AND your other device, such as your mobile.
Hard drive	Hard disk, flash disk, Hard disk drive (HDD), Solid State Drive (SSD)	The part of your device that stores your data. Generally, this is internal to your device, e.g. built in, as opposed to an External USB Drive, for example.
USB Drive	Pen drive, USB stick, External hard drive, Flash drive	A hard drive data external to your device. For example, you can copy data, such as pictures, from your computer's hard drive to a USB drive to give to your friend.
Format	Wipe, scrub, delete	The process of deleting all data from your Hard Drive. Be aware that formatting a hard drive will not securely remove the data; for example, a thief may still be able to retrieve your data.

Term	Also known as	Description
Denial of Service	DOS, Distributed Denial of Service, DDOS	A piece of computer software; normally a virus, that unites with other similarly infected devices and attacks websites or companies by bombarding them with data to such an extent, their systems shut down under the strain.
Backup	Archive	Taking a copy of the data on your hard disk or device, such as your important documents or pictures and storing them in an alternative location in the event your computer or device is lost or damaged.
Dark web	Tor (NB: Tor can be, and is, used legitimately, but unfortunately it is also used for illegitimate means).	An area of the Internet sealed off and unpublished on Search Engines like Google and Bing. A majority of the websites and data on the Dark Web are illegal. You can't stumble into the Dark Web, you need to know how to get there, so don't worry too much about it.
Social Engineering		A mean of extracting important or secure information from you by manipulating a conversation with you and acting upon your trust, or knowledge of you. Generally used by criminals to extort money.
False Positive		This is when a file or email is recognised as a virus or SPAM, when it fact, it is legitimate. Normally, if this happens, you can mark the file or email as safe.
Trolling	Online abuse, cyber bullying	Offensive and harassing comments made online. This can be via any form of communication, such as email, chat or social media. Do not tolerate it – report it and block it.

Home Network Diagram

To gain some context around our discussions on Online Security, a simple diagram and an explanation about how devices connect to Wi-Fi and the Internet is below:

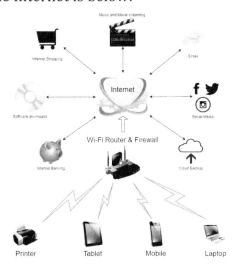

Figure - A typical home Wi-Fi set-up

Generally speaking, each home will have a set-up like the above.

Your PC or Mac (seen above as a laptop), along with any tablet and mobile phone devices, and possibly your printer, will connect to a Wi-Fi network. Each device connecting your home network can access one another. This is why your wireless laptop can print to your wireless printer.

The Wi-Fi router provides your Wi-Fi network and 'routes' your connected devices onto the Internet so you can download movies, see your bank account, order your groceries and post on social media.

People or devices outside of your Wi-Fi network (e.g. those on the Internet) cannot see or connect to your laptops, mobiles, etc. This is known as a firewall.

When you access something from the Internet you 'pull' it; it is not 'pushed' or sent to you. For example, when you access a web page, you pull it, or download it to your computer. Even your email is not sent to you, even though this is how it appears. What actually happens is you pull, or download your email from the Internet equivalent of a post box.

Why am I telling you this? The moral of the story is that no one can push a virus onto your device - you have to download it. No one can access to your computer - you have to allow them access, or download a virus to allow them to do this. At all times, you're in control of what you do and don't install on your devices, and who you do and don't let access them.

This is an over generalisation. The truth is more complex, but we needn't worry about this for now. As long as you exercise common sense, and follow good advice, you will remain safe online.

The Key Lessons

We'll open with a collection of the Key Lessons. These complete each chapter as a summary, but are useful as a quick reference to remember or keep close to hand.

Scams by phone

- Consider scams online or on the phone as you would at your door, or on the street. If someone knocked on your door and asked for £50 would you give it to them? Likewise, you wouldn't give a stranger your bank card and PIN code if they asked for it. Use your instincts and question whether the person calling you is genuine or not.
- No one will ever call you saying your computer is slow or has a virus. This is a scam. Hang up immediately. Consider blocking anonymous or international numbers to reduce the amount of unwelcome calls.
- Don't be afraid to challenge someone calling you and ask them to prove they are who they say they are. If they can't prove it, but say the matter is urgent, ask them for other options, such as visiting your local branch or sending a letter or an email.

Scams by email

- If you receive a message via email, SMS text, Skype, Facebook, WhatsApp, or any similar messaging services from someone you don't recognise, or if the content looks suspicious or doesn't make sense (e.g. an email from a hotel you've never booked), then DELETE THE MESSAGE.

- If you receive a message that looks suspicious, but you would like peace of mind, then contact the organisation where the email is from. Contact them by phone or a new email - do not reply to the suspicious looking email.
- Be wary of emails with links or attachments, or with peculiar subject lines. Check if the email is legitimate by hovering over, or clicking the sender's name - you will be able to tell it is illegitimate if the company's name doesn't appear.

SPAM

- Don't give your email address to anyone you don't want to email you. This includes publishing your email address on social media or on a website.
- If you do complete a form where you must give your email address, ensure you've checked (or unchecked) the privacy options about what the company will do with your email.
- Do not attempt to unsubscribe from SPAM. Instead, mark it as SPAM or 'Junk' and let your email service or programme sweep it up.
- Consider two email addresses, one for friends, family and important correspondence, and another for marketing, mailing lists, etc.

Viruses

- Everyone has either caught a computer virus or come close to getting one, the same way we've all experienced being scammed in some shape or form. Don't worry, don't panic - as we've already said, there are bad people out there trying to scam you online, like there are on the street. Don't be afraid to go out, or online, just exercise caution and awareness.
- Do not open any attachments on emails you do not recognise.

- Do not open any attachments a web page tries to download on your behalf.
- If you get an email from a friend you were not expecting, or contains peculiar content, then check the address of the email carefully, or contact them to make sure they haven't been hacked.
- If you depend on your machine or device for business, I would recommend paying for Anti-Virus. It's still worth considering if you use your computer a lot or perform Internet Banking, for example.
- Be aware of the types of viruses and scams. Newspapers and national news often carry coverage of threats such as widespread virus outbreaks or scams. This will, unfortunately, become more common as the digital age evolves, so keep yourself informed.

Genuine Software and the Dangers of Next, Next, I Accept, Finish

- Don't click 'Next, Next, I Accept, Finish' without knowing what you're accepting. Check the software you're installing, the same way you'd check a contract or stranger who wanted to sell you something.
- Purchase and use genuine software from trusted locations. Check software is genuine when it's installing.

Staying Safe Online

- You wouldn't walk into a random building that proclaimed to represent your bank and hand them your money for depositing. You'd want to make sure it was your bank. Make sure the websites you give your money or details to are genuine by looking for the padlock symbol.
- If a web site starts behaving in a way you don't like or didn't expect, then close it or reboot your computer.

- It's incredibly rare (almost impossible if you're running the latest Anti-Virus and patches on your computer) to get a virus just by accessing a web site. However, if the website forces you to download a file or prompts you to 'Accept' something you didn't ask for then close it and re-boot your machine.
- On your social media accounts, check your privacy settings - make sure you're not advertising to the world what you're up to.

Servicing your computer

- Get rid of your XP machine. You may be attached to it, or can't afford to buy a new one, but it could prove costlier to keep it. If you do have XP and insist on keeping it, then I would advise against connecting it to the Internet or plugging in any USB drives to keep it safe.
- If your machine wants to update itself, let it - don't put it off.
- Do not let anyone access your computer who you don't trust.
- Learn to recognise how your computer behaves and acts. If strange prompts, or messages start appearing, and you think something is wrong, then follow your gut and assume something is wrong. Run Anti-Virus scans and updates. Get some help if you're worried.

PINs and Passwords

- Use complex passwords. Yes, they are annoying to remember, but it's less annoying than finding someone has hacked your account and spent all your money.
- If you do need to write your passwords down, then do so securely. It's not a myth that people write their passwords on a Post-It and stick them on their monitors. Would you leave a spare key in your latch, or write your pin on your bank card?

- If your password is hacked or guessed, then change it and never use it again.
- If you store your passwords in a file on your computer, secure the file as best as possible by putting a password on it and obscuring it as much as possible.
- If you feel confident enough, consider setting up Multi-Factor Authentication (MFA) on your most critical services, e.g. email. MFA will not 100% guarantee safety (nothing is 100% safe) but it will make it very, very difficult for someone to access your account.

Backups and the Cloud

- If it's important to you, back it up!
- The question I ask most is: 'If your computer caught fire right now and you lost all your files, what would you do?' If the answer is: 'I'd lose all my data and it would be a disaster', then back up your files.
- If you do back up to 'The Cloud', remember to ensure the Cloud service you are using has a complex password, and consider using Multi-Factor Authentication.

1 Scams by phone

Although not technically online, telephone scams are a good place for us to start. Most of us will have experienced a phone call asking for some information or trying to sell us something. We're often overly polite (I think it's a British thing), keeping the person who is either trying to sell us or scam us, on the phone. We often end up apologising to them. There is one simple method to get rid of them:

HANG UP!

A common scam these days is to receive a call purporting to be from your software or Internet provider, informing you that you have a virus or your Internet is slow. **This is a scam**. The scammer's intention is to ask you to check some details on your computer, then grant them access. When the scammer has access, they lock down your computer and ask for money to fix it. I have received such a call and led them on (this is not advisable) to see what would happen. I obviously stopped at the point before they got access to my computer, but it allowed me to understand how genuine it would appear to someone who wasn't familiar with computers. I can see why people get tricked.

We do get genuine calls, but there are some basic ways to sort the goodies from the baddies.

Basic

a) No one will ever call you telling you your computer is slow or has a virus - if you get a call like this: HANG UP - do not talk to them, do not explain anything - HANG UP.

b) No one legitimate will ever call you and ask for your password, bank account/credit card details, or access to your computer. If you call your computer support company, they may need access to your computer, but remember: you called them asking for help, they will not call you asking if you want help.

c) Contact your telephone provider, e.g. BT, Virgin, etc. and ask what services they offer to block unwelcome calls. Screening services are available to sort trusted callers from unknown callers.

d) Telephone providers can also block international numbers from calling (clearly, this isn't useful if you receive international calls).

e) You could also ask your telephone provider to block anonymous calls. If friends or family who call you block their number, this can be released so they can still ring you. For example, on BT, the caller dials 1470 before making the call to release their number.

f) Consider the Telephone Preference Service (TPS - Search for them online). This is a free service. You fill out a form, which is meant to exclude you from sales calls. It doesn't always work, but it's a start. If you're hassled by the same number, you can use the TPS to report them. Companies can be fined for unsolicited calls.

g) No one will call you asking for money to block unwelcome calls. It may sound tempting to pay £30 and have all marketing and fraudulent calls stopped, but this is a scam in itself. Always speak to your telephone provider and ask for options. If someone claims they can offer you this service, then hang up.

h) Do not feel guilty asking the caller to further identify themselves. If someone is genuine, they won't mind providing proof or they will provide you options to make you feel safe. A fraudster will get angry and aggressive if you challenge them - a certain way to know they are fake and your prompt to hang up the phone.

Intermediate

i) If you have been the victim of a scam, or there is a security issue on your account, your bank should send you a message asking for you to call them. For example, when someone cloned my card, and tried to spend £800, I received an automated message from my bank asking me to check my transactions. When I saw an £800 spend I never made, instructions were provided on how to contact my bank. If you are unsure, call the bank on the number provided on your bank statement or back of your credit card.

j) If you are a mobile phone user, look for apps that block unwelcome calls. Apps like these maintain a list of unwelcome companies and either diverts them to voicemail or 'call-drops' them. A 'call-drop' is when the phone is immediately answered and hung up. The result is the call isn't even directed to voicemail.

k) You can manually block numbers yourself on your mobile. This varies from provider to provider so research how to do this.

Advanced

l) Some devices can be installed into your home to filter and block unwelcome calls. Be careful about how these devices are implemented to ensure you still receive the calls you want.

m) If you use Telephone Banking, beware of this scam: someone will call you, pretending to be from your bank. They ask you to call the bank back and either give you a fake number or use a telephone trick to keep the line open. Getting you to dial a fake number or keeping the line open allows the fraudsters to highjack your telephone banking details and passwords, possibly giving them access to your account. If you get such a call, consider dialling back from another phone or research the correct number to ring - you can use a search engine, like Google or Bing to do this. Even consider going into your local branch. Do not enter automated details or pass-words into a machine if you are unsure - ask to speak to someone and get them to prove who they are.

Key Lessons

- Consider scams online or on the phone as you would at your door, or on the street. If someone knocked on your door and asked for £50 would you give it to them? Like-wise, you wouldn't give a stranger your bank card and PIN code if they asked for it. Use your instincts and question whether the person calling you is genuine or not.
- No one will ever call you saying your computer is slow or has a virus. This is a scam. Hang up immediately. Consider blocking anonymous or international numbers to reduce the amount of unwelcome calls.
- Don't be afraid to challenge someone calling you and ask them to prove they are who they say they are. If they can't prove it, but say the matter is urgent, ask them for other options, such as visiting your local branch or sending a letter or an email.

2 Scams by email

Just as fraudsters and criminals will use the phone to scam you, emails are another tactic. Email scams can be very clever. However, a similar principle applies to suspect emails as it does to suspect phone calls. If you don't recognise the email, or something looks suspicious:

DELETE IT

Here's an example of something sinister - an email from a hotel I've never booked or stayed at, informing me I owe them money. Their trick is to scare me into opening the attachment - the attachment is not all it seems (I nearly fell for it, so don't be embarrassed - it can happen to anyone):

Booking Confirmation / WH401 http://theyaf.com/booking-confirmation wh401xq9-1901201/.pdf Click or tap to follow link.

We are pleased to confirm your reservation and look forward Park Avenue Hotel. You will find your booking details below. Please print booking confirmation and present at reception when checking in.

Reference: WH401XQ9

Arrival Date 20 Jan 2017
Departure Date 22 Jan 2017
Check In Time 02:00 PM to 11:30 PM

Figure - Attachments and Links might not be what they proclaim to be

You will see the email has a link, asking me to check my booking confirmation. Most email programs will allow you to check which website the link is sending you to by hovering over the text in the link. In the example above, the link tried to send me to a website that looked completely unrelated. It's very likely this link was a link to a virus or scam or some sort.

A similar scam manifests as an email from the HMRC, informing you that a rebate is due - it can be quite enticing thinking the tax man is about to return some of your money. But think for a minute. The HMRC would never send you a message telling you the amount owed to you. The HMRC, like many banks and financial companies, will send you an email saying there is a message waiting on your account.

A genuine email will not contain links for you to click, or attachments for you to download.

Basic

a) If you receive an email and you don't know who it is from, or what it is about, then DELETE IT. Most of the time you will know what the email is, e.g. information about your online grocery shop, a mailing list you've knowingly sub-scribed to, or an email from a family or friend.

b) Look for typos, poor English and grammar. Invariably, scammers don't practise good English, and words, sen-tences, etc. can look peculiar - everyone is prone to the odd smelling mistake, but exercise caution when it's something you don't immediately recognise.

c) Emails can look like they're from someone you trust, e.g. a friend or family member, your bank or shopping compa-ny. However, the content of the email may look odd. If you see a strange looking link or message, it may not genuine. If you're unsure, contact the person who sent you the email by writing a new email or calling them. Do not reply to the suspect email.

d) Most email programs let you check the sender's actual email address by hovering over, or clicking on it - this will help you identify whether it's real or not, for example, this email is not from *Aldi* - note the actual email of screwball@random chain of letters:

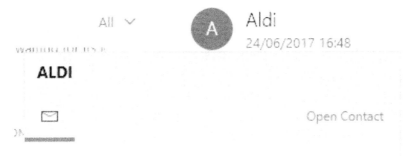

All ∨   A   Aldi
24/06/2017 16:48

ALDI

✉   Open Contact

Personal: screwball@IApArOhYsTeRoPeXy.CfF6.pRoT

e) If a friend or family member sends you a joke or image that looks suspicious and doesn't feel right, then ring them or email them and ask them if they meant to. It may be their account has been hacked and they need to be informed. Equally, it may be that they forwarded you some chain mail or a scam - in this case, call them and ask them if they meant to send it to you.

f) Be wary of attachments in emails, especially if you don't recognise them. Random banks and hotels will never email you an invoice or statement in error. If you really need to be sure, then research the hotel, bank, shop, etc. and call them to ask.

g) Final warnings, or very urgent and important correspondence, will rarely arrive via email. If you haven't paid your electricity bill, you are more likely to receive a letter, rather than an email. Remember, if you're unsure, then call the company in question. If you are about to be disconnected, they will be able to tell you. The scam email is intended to scare you in the hope you'll open the link or attachment.

h) Make sure your computer has up to date Anti-Virus software - viruses within emails can be stopped by a good AV program, but not always. Do not rely on your Anti-virus software to stop everything. Exercising that all important gut-feeling may be more powerful.

2.1 Not just email

Today, we might receive messages in a variety of ways, not just through email. Scam messages can be received on SMS text messages, Skype, Facebook, WhatsApp, etc. - each time the scam message will purport to be urgent or from someone you know, or asking you to call a number or click a link you don't recognise - follow the same rule:

If you don't recognise the message, its content or who it's from: DELETE IT.

Key Lessons

- If you receive a message via email, SMS text, Skype, Facebook, WhatsApp, or any similar messaging services from someone you don't recognise, or if the content looks suspicious or doesn't make sense (e.g. an email from a hotel you've never booked), then DELETE THE MESSAGE.
- If you receive a message that looks suspicious, but you would like peace of mind, then contact the organisation where the email is from. Contact them by phone or a new email - do not reply to the suspicious looking email.
- Be wary of emails with links or attachments, or with peculiar subject lines. Check if the email is legitimate by hovering over, or clicking the sender's name - you will be able to tell it is illegitimate if the company's name doesn't appear.

3 SPAM

Entire books can be (and probably have been) written about SPAM. SPAM is unsolicited email, e.g. email you haven't asked for, and is illegal. SPAM emails aren't always scams, but the intention is to get something from you, e.g. to make you buy a product.

Basic

What is the difference between SPAM and legitimate emails?

The question is: did you ask for it? If you registered on mailing list, or elected to receive emails from a company, then it's not SPAM. If a company or person emails you out of the blue, and you haven't asked for it, then it is SPAM.

However, often you may have registered to receive emails inadvertently. For example, if you visit a site, or buy a product, or even complete a paper form which has your email address on it, be sure to read the section about receiving information from the company or third-parties.

If you tick the box, or sometimes leave it unticked (this is why it's confusing and you need to read what your options are), you may be agreeing to receive emails from the company and any unknown third-parties.

The good news is: if you register with a legitimate company, you can unsubscribe from their email list. There is normally an option to do this within the email.

If you can't unsubscribe, or if you keep receiving emails after you've unsubscribed, then the email is considered illegal and you can report the company. See the 'Useful Website' section later for how to do this.

Why do companies SPAM us?

There is a simple reason: it works. If a SPAMMER sends a million emails, it only takes one person to buy from them to have made the SPAM successful. You'd be surprised how often this happens.

How do SPAMMERS acquire our email addresses?

There are lots of answers to this:

a) You've advertised your email, for example, on a website or on social media. Companies trawl the internet looking for email addresses to harvest. Why? Because they can sell lists of harvested emails to SPAMMERs.

b) Your email address has been illegally sold or stolen from a legitimate company who had your email address. There's not a great deal you can do about this, other than decide whether you want to deal with such a company in the future.

c) Your email address has been guessed. If you wanted to guess a list of email addresses, you might start with john.smith@email.com - how many other obvious email addresses can you think of in a minute? Now think what a computer could do if it had a telephone directory of names?

How do I distinguish SPAM from legitimate emails?

There is no exact science - remember that all important gut feeling? That's your best weapon. Here are some ways that will help:

a) Did you ask for the email? For example, is the email from a shop or company you've recently purchased from? Did you give them your email, or get asked if you'd like an e-receipt?

b) Do you recognise the company or product? If the product is less than savoury or you have no idea what it is, then it's probably SPAM.
c) Is the title inappropriate in trying allure you to open the email? Ask yourself whether a legitimate company would employ this method.
d) Is the spelling or the grammar within the email poor? Any marketing email or document with spelling mistakes should be questioned.

Do	Don't
Protect the security of your email address like you would your personal details, such as home address or mobile phone.	Advertise your email address on social media or online. Would you post your home address on Facebook or Twitter?
Distinguish from illegal SPAM and email mailing lists you have signed up for. You can unsub-scribe from email marketing lists – you can't from SPAM.	Unsubscribe from illegal SPAM. If you do this, you're confirming your email address is active and you'll get more SPAM.
Consider having two email accounts – one for email marketing lists and one for friends and family.	Buy anything or respond to anything on a SPAM email. It could be a scam or a virus.
Consider having a difficult to guess email address. For example, instead of your name, use a nick name.	Ignore the email marketing privacy questions. Make sure you read them carefully and tick or untick according to your choice.
Use your email service or programme's Junk Filter. Add unwanted emails into your Junk or report them as SPAM in the email programme. The software will learn what you identify as SPAM and start to block it.	Hand over your email address without asking why someone wants it. There are lots of reasons you might want someone to email you and plenty of reasons why you don't. It's your choice.

e) Is the email actually from the company, or has it been spoofed (as in the example above)? Hover over the email address, or click on the sender's name to see whether it's from the company, or instead, a spurious list of letters and numbers.

How you can prevent and stop SPAM. Some do's and don'ts:

What if the SPAM keeps coming?

I was asked how to stop SPAM altogether. Unfortunately, unless you have access to a very expensive email monitoring system (such as large organisations have), you are limited to adding SPAM into your Junk folder and hoping your email service or programme does the rest.

The problem is, once the SPAMMERs have your email address, they won't let it go. Even if you don't respond, or block them, they will keep sending it. Remember, while there are people behind the SPAM, it's computers with massive lists of email addresses that process your address and send you the SPAM. The computers don't care that you aren't responding, they just keep sending, and the people behind the system hope that one will get through.

While Internet authorities and providers can identify SPAM systems and shut them down, it is very easy to set one up elsewhere (and even easier where Internet regulation is lacking).

There is an alternative, but it is quite drastic: Set-up a new email account

Armed with a new email account, you can tell your family and friends to start using it for correspondence and gradually move any services, like banking, shopping, etc. to it. You can keep your old email account and check it from time to time for any emails you might want, or (as suggested earlier) keep the old one for marketing messages and your new one for main and important correspondence. Just remember to keep the new one safe and don't share its details.

3.1 Scams vs. SPAM? Viruses, Ransomware and Phishing

I was asked what was the difference between email scams and SPAM.

Generally speaking, SPAM will try and sell you something and a scam will try and steal something. However it's not always that simple. SPAM, scams and viruses can appear within email with different intentions. I have listed some of them below. This won't necessarily help stop you being scammed or infected with a virus, but it may help you understand the rationale:

a) SPAM - Unsolicited emails will generally try and sell you something, but can also contain unwanted nasties that will bombard you with adverts and emails.

b) VIRUS - If you receive an email with an attachment that you don't recognise, it could be someone trying to infect your machine with a virus. It's unlikely you have been specifically targeted. Like SPAM, virus emails are sent in-discriminately. What damage can a virus do?

    i. RANSOMWARE - you may have heard this phrase more and more. A Ransomware virus will infect your machine and lock you out of your files and software, then demand money for them to be returned.

    ii. KEYLOGGER - A Keylogger virus will infect your system and record your activity, e.g. the keys you press, the programs you load, the websites you visit, etc. The virus will then send this recorded data to someone on the Internet who will know, for example, which bank you use and how to log in and get your money.

    iii. BOT - A Bot is a virus that can turn your machine into a slave and place it under its master's command (normally the virus creator). The bot remains dormant, e.g. you may be unaware of its presence (unlike Ransomware which demands cash overtly). If a virus creator can infect millions of machines, they can turn them into a weapon of sorts to attack organisations - normally known as a Distributed Denial of Service attack.

Opening an infected email attachment could infect your computer, simply looking at the email (e.g. opening the email, but not opening the attachment) should be OK. However, it is still safer to delete an email you don't recognise without opening it.

c) PHISHING - This technique attempts to trick you into entering your personal details onto a site that is fake. For example, you may receive an email that looks like it is from your bank. It has the same logo, branding, etc. It tells you that you have a problem with your account and asks you to click a link to fix the problem. The link takes you to a site that looks like your bank, so you enter your account number, sort code, password, etc. - the site however is fake and now the scammer has your details and access to your account.

d) DESTRUCTION - I've recently added this because a virus hit in June 2017 called Petya. Petya looked like Ransomware, but on further investigation, it turned out the virus's sole purpose was to destroy data and cause chaos. No money, no blackmail - just disruption. Some people and companies affected found their files destroyed beyond repair and had to restore from a back-up.

Viruses don't always arrive via email. There are other ways they can infect your system, but remember, you are in control of whether this happens or not. Being vigilant, following the advice in this guide and maintaining your computer can make it very difficult for your machine to be infected.

3.1.1 SPAM or Virus?

I thought it would be useful to provide an example of SPAM and a virus on an email. Below is a perfect example; if anything for its comedic value.

Tue 11/03/2014 13:11

Mavis Fletcher <recapsz75@rowemcgill.com>

Unpaid penalty #3465656

To   Andrew Perry

Retention Policy   Junk Email (30 days)   Expires   10/04/2014

This item will expire in 29 days. To keep this item longer apply a different Retention Policy

Links and other functionality have been disabled in this message. To turn on that functionality, move this message to the Inbox.
This message was marked as spam using a junk filter other than the Outlook Junk E-mail filter.
Outlook blocked access to the following potentially unsafe attachments: Report.zip, ATT00001.txt.

Dear Sir/Madam!

You have the surcharges for utilities.
The report is in the attached ZIP-file.
You gotta revise it before May 6th 2014. Your login: SFP/27283.
Otherwise you'll obtain additional punishment.

All the best, chief of Police station #34.

Figure - if it wasn't for the serious nature of SPAM and Viruses, this illegitimate email would be funny

Apparently, I need to pay the 'chief of Police station #34' a surcharge for 'utilities'. Quite why I owe these surcharges, or why the Chief of Police is following this up, is beyond me. However, this email has all the hallmarks of SPAM and rather likely, a virus.

Let's play SPAM and Virus bingo:

a) Is the sender unknown to me? Yes - maybe you know someone call Mavis Fletcher. I don't.
b) Is the sender's email address peculiar looking or unrecognisable? Yes - a strange combination of letters that don't make sense.
c) Is the subject line provocative? Yes - 'Unpaid Penalty' would get most people's hackles up.
d) Does the email have an attachment? Yes - my email program blocked the attachment, and furthermore recognised it was SPAM and added it to my 'Junk' folder.

e) Does the email ask me to do something or open something? Yes - I have to pay a penalty which I'll find in the attached ZIP file.

f) Does the email have odd spelling and grammar? Yes - a formal notice from the police, or notice asking me to pay a fine is unlikely to use terms like 'gotta', or sign off 'all the best'.

You may not be surprised to hear I didn't respond to the Chief of Police station #34, nor did I open their attachment. I never heard from them again...

Key Lessons

- Don't give your email address to anyone you don't want to email you. This includes publishing your email address on social media or on a website.
- If you do complete a form where you must give your email address, ensure you've checked (or unchecked) the privacy options about what the company will do with your email.
- Do not attempt to unsubscribe from SPAM. Instead, mark it as SPAM or 'Junk' and let your email service or programme sweep it up.
- Consider two email addresses, one for friends, family and important correspondence, and another for marketing, mailing lists, etc.

4 Viruses

Viruses are computer software designed with a purpose, like a word-processor is used to write documents, or a photo editor used to brighten up your pictures. The difference with a virus is its intention - it is not designed to help you. Instead it will try to damage your computer or attempt to get your details and money.

As we've seen, viruses come in different shapes and forms. There are ways to protect yourself, but nothing is fool proof. This section explains about viruses and how to protect yourself.

Basic

4.1 Anti-Virus

It's a common question: do I need to pay for Anti-virus?

If you have a Windows machine, it will come with free anti-virus. For day to day Internet browsing, this is generally OK. If you want extra safety or if you run Internet banking, then getting an advanced anti-virus program is a good idea. If you run a business, I would say it's vital.

The question I ask is: how much do you trust the emails you receive or the sites you visit? And how valuable is your computer to you?

A good example is when I spoke to a self-employed trader. His computer was his main mechanism for dealing with his clients. He received lots of emails from lots of different people, e.g. those he didn't know he could trust.

I said: "For £25 a year, it's good insurance." All it would take is a rogue email from an address that manifested as a new client and his machine could be taken off line, losing him thousands of pounds in business - the maths add up.

However, if you only ever email your cousin in Australia, look at the same one or two web sites, or if your computer goes wrong, you survive without it, then you can probably save that £25.

4.2 The day I got a virus

To prove it can happen to anyone; even someone who has worked in IT all his life, has helped others with computer security and consider myself fairly switched on when it comes to scams, etc., I thought it might be helpful to explain how, a few years back, I got a virus.

One morning, I switched on my computer. As Windows connected to the Internet, it asked me to update a program called Flash Player (a common program on most machines used to play videos in your Internet browser). I was in a rush, so I postponed the update.

Later that evening, I switched my machine back on and was browsing the Internet. I was researching how to fix a problem and went to a website I hadn't visited before. I received a message saying I had to update Flash. Because I'd seen the update earlier that day, I clicked Update. And (probably because it was late and I was tired), I clicked all the Next, Next, Next, Yes, 'I accept' prompts without reading them (we discuss this later).

Next thing, I start getting very strange errors. Then messages asking for money appeared.

What happened? This was partly due to bad luck. Because the genuine Flash Update appeared that morning, I assumed the one that night was genuine - it wasn't. It was a fake Flash Update that contained a virus. The main fault was mine however, because I didn't bother to check the web site and that the update was genuine.

Why didn't my Anti-Virus software identify the virus? Good question. The honest answer is, I don't know. All I can say is that I was running a free Anti-Virus program on that laptop. Would a paid Anti-Virus program have identified the virus? I don't know, but possibly.

What did I do? First thing was to disconnect my laptop from the wireless network and Internet - this stopped the virus communicating with my other devices on my network, the Internet (and possibly Virus creator).

How did I do this? In my case, my laptop had a Wi-Fi switch that deactivated Wi-Fi (and hence my connection to the Internet). Other machines have a Flight Mode, which will do the same. Others might be connected with a cable, which can be unplugged. If in doubt, turn off your Internet router and then find out how to enable Flight Mode or disable Wi-Fi.

What next? A long story, too detailed for this guide. However, about four hours later, I unpicked the virus and removed it from my system. This was no mean feat, believe me. I was close to clearing all the data (formatting) my laptop and restoring files from backup, reinstalling applications, etc., which would have taken a day at least.

What could I have done differently? I should have checked whether this was a genuine Flash install. This isn't always obvious, but there is a way to check if a program is genuine or not. There are several types of viruses - this one masqueraded as a genuine update and fooled me, yet if I'd have been on my toes, I could have prevented it.

What's the moral of the story? Updates to your computer are important (see the next few chapters), but should be performed in a trusted and recognised manner. If you get a random pop up requesting you update your machine, you should exercise caution - I was caught out partly through circumstance, partly through tiredness, but mainly through complacency.

I wouldn't blame anyone in the slightest if they got caught out by a sophisticated scam or virus, but there are things you can do to keep yourself safe.

4.3 Protecting yourself against viruses

a) Make sure you have a good and up to date Anti-Virus programme (more on this later).
b) Make sure you update and patch your computer (more on this later too).
c) Be cautious of seemingly random messages, telling you to run updates. Learn to trust and recognise the main updates, like Windows or Mac Updates, for example.
d) When you install a new program, check it is from a valid source and publisher - you will get an option to do this (we discuss more about this later)
e) Make sure you download or acquire software from safe locations, e.g. the software producer's website. Some dishonest websites masquerade as genuine, offering software for reduced costs or free. Some shops or stalls may also offer tempting deals for software - remember: there is no such thing as a free lunch.
f) Keep good backups of your files (lots more on this later).

4.4 If you think you might have a virus:

a) Disconnect your machine from the Internet - most machines have a switch to deactivate Wi-Fi or enable Flight Mode.
b) If possible, use another computer, or a friend's, to research what the virus is. Most Anti-Virus producers offer software that runs from a USB disk that can remove the virus from your machine.
c) Get help from a reliable source. This isn't always possible, at least quickly or cheaply, but if you're not comfortable with tackling the virus, it would be better to get help from someone who can help. DO NOT pay any ransom or make contact with the virus makers.
d) It may be that you have to wipe (also known as format, factory reset or clean install) your machine of all files and start again - not something I would recommend without some help. This is annoying, but if you've kept good backups and a record of all your passwords, etc. then it may be the only way to completely eradicate the virus from your machine.

4.5 Scams and viruses on Macs, mobiles and tablets

It's a myth Apple machines don't get viruses. In fact, one of the most curious jobs I ever worked on was a network of Apple Mac computers which had been failing on and off for months. I checked all the obvious signs, but nothing added up.

Until I asked: "do you have Anti-Virus software?"

"But Macs don't get viruses, do they?" was the response.

We installed some Anti-Virus software and found the whole network was infested with a virus, which was causing the stability problems.

The main reason Windows machines are more susceptible to viruses is because there are more of them, e.g. most large organisations use Windows as their main operating system. It makes sense for a virus author to target the largest attack base and increase their chances of infection.

Viruses on phones and tablets are less common, but that doesn't make them less susceptible. Indeed, like Macs, they are not immune. If you do pay for anti-virus software, you might get phone or tablet Anti-virus bundled in. Is it worth it? Again, it's insurance. If your phone is your life blood (and these days, it is for a lot of people), then it's worth looking at your options.

Free anti-virus software is available, but this will pester you to buy the full version or create lots of adverts - if you can handle these, then it's worth considering as a half-way house between the in-built Anti-virus and the paid-for version. It's certainly better than nothing.

4.6 Adware

Adware is similar to a virus in that you don't want it on your machine. In general, it's less destructive or harmful, but this isn't always the case.

If you've ever seen advertising banners (pop-ups) or buttons appearing in your Internet browser that you didn't ask for, or if you're constantly directed to sites you didn't click on, then it's likely to be adware. Adware can also slow your machine down. If anyone asks me why their machine is slow, adware is one of the first places I look.

At best, adware will be an annoyance; at worst, it will collect information about your Internet browsing habits (such as which Internet Banking service you use) and send it to someone.

Some Anti-Virus programmes will identify and remove adware, or you can search for adware removal tools. If you do run an adware scan on your machine, it can take a number of hours as it needs to check every file on your machine. It can be worth the wait however.

Key Lessons

- Everyone has either caught a computer virus or come close to getting one, the same way we've all experienced being scammed in some shape or form. Don't worry, don't panic - as we've already said, there are bad people out there trying to scam you online, like there are on the street. Don't be afraid to go out, or online, just exercise caution and awareness.
- Do not open any attachments on emails you do not recognise.
- Do not open any attachments a web page tries to download on your behalf.
- If you get an email from a friend you were not expecting, or contains peculiar content, then check the address of the email carefully, or contact them to make sure they haven't been hacked.
- If you depend on your machine or device for business, I would recommend paying for Anti-Virus. It's still worth considering if you use your computer a lot or perform Internet Banking, for example.

- Be aware of the types of viruses and scams. Newspapers and national news often carry coverage of threats such as widespread virus outbreaks or scams. This will, unfortunately, become more common as the digital age evolves, so keep yourself informed.

5 Genuine Software and the dangers of Next, Next, I Accept, Finish

As we saw in the last chapter, some software will masquerade as genuine when it is, in fact, a virus. Unfortunately, it's not easy to check what is genuine and what is fake software.

Basic

There are some basic ways to check the software you're installing is genuine:

a) Purchase your software from a valid source. This might be from a high-street store, or from an online store. An online store would be a recognisable brand, such as Google, Microsoft, Apple or Adobe. A high street store should be instantly recognisable -be wary of cheap deals at markets stalls.

b) Don't accept copied or pirated software from people. Normally, this software has been altered in some way to override the copyright. Sometimes, viruses are snuck into the software too.

There is another method, however it is a little more complex and possibly belongs in the 'Intermediate' difficulty section. However, it is worth taking a look. Don't worry if you find it too technical, just be aware of your options.

5.1 Checking software is what it says it is

A modern Windows computer will prompt you each time you install some software. Often, we (me included) skip these prompts - they are important however. You may recognise the 'User Access Control' message below (particularly the bit on the left):

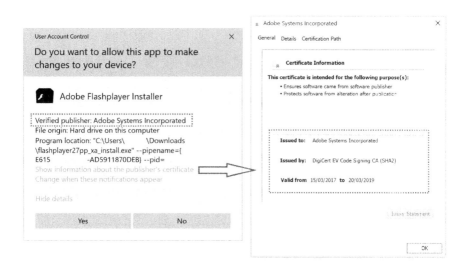

Figure - Before you install software,
check it is from a legitimate source

This prompt will tell you who the software is from (the bit highlighted). In this case we can see the application is from a legitimate provider, Adobe. If the 'Verified Publisher' says 'Unknown' or looks obscure then raise your suspicion level and consider selecting 'No', which will cancel the install. I wish I had done this when I got my virus…

My immediate advice is: if you try to install a program and the Verified Publisher is 'Unknown' or unrelated to the program you're installing, e.g. it doesn't say Google, Microsoft, Apple, etc. then CANCEL the installation and get some advice. Legitimate software will always have a recognisable 'Verified Publisher' you can trace or research.

5.2 Dangers of Next, Next, I accept, Finish

We're all in a hurry, aren't we? We don't have time to read disclaimers, small print or bother with all these boring software prompts. This is what some illegitimate (and some legitimate) software companies rely on.

How often have you clicked Next, Next, I accept, Finish? How often have you wondered where that new icon came from, or why your browser's homepage starts logging onto another site? Often the two questions are related.

Illegitimate software will encourage you to install extra software or 'plug-ins' - why? Because, at best, they make money from bundling other companies' software with theirs. At worst, someone is trying to sneak something scary onto your machine, like a virus.

Even recognised software brands will attempt to persuade you to use their search engine or to install something onto your machine that hooks you into their software or company. Sometimes this is OK, sometimes not... the point is: it's your choice.

My advice: don't just click Next, Next, I accept, Finish. Look out for any options that ask you if you'd like to change your home page, or install a tool you weren't expecting. If you want them, great! If you don't, unselect the offending offer and carry on. If a piece of software tries to install something against your will, then it's probably not something you'd want on your computer anyway.

Intermediate

If you really want to check who this 'Verified Publisher' is, you can click 'Show information about the publisher's certificate' - this brings up the bit on the right (from the above image). You can inspect information about the program's publisher and confirm they are legitimate.

A virus company or suspect software provider will not have a certificate of authenticity and Windows will warn you of this.

Key Lessons

- Don't click 'Next, Next, I Accept, Finish' without knowing what you're accepting. Check the software you're installing, the same way you'd check a contract or stranger who wanted to sell you something.
- Purchase and use genuine software from trusted locations. Check software is genuine when it's installing.

6 Staying safe online

These days, everything is online. Banking, council services, grocery shopping, tickets for transport, concerts and event. It's becoming harder to stay offline, as more and more companies force us onto their websites.

Like phone scams, email scams and rogue software, it is hard to distinguish what is good from what is bad. Likewise, as we saw with Phishing scams, it is possible to be tricked into accessing a website that claims to be legitimate, but is far from it. How do we know?

Basic

6.1 Websites: Sorting the good from the bad

An easy to follow rule is:

Never buy anything, or enter any payment or password details into a site that is not secure.

How can you tell? The simple way is in your browser, for example, Chrome, Internet Explorer, Safari, etc. Legitimate sites that ask for money or sell products will have a padlock symbol. Your browser will show them in slightly different ways, but there will always be a padlock.

*Figure - Never enter confidential information
into a website without a padlock*

The padlock symbol means the website is secure and has been validated by an independent 'Certificate Authority' - this sounds complex, but don't worry - all you need to know is that the site is safe. Some sites will even appear in a nice green shade to make it easier to spot.

More on padlocks and these 'Certificate Authorities' later.

6.2 Rogue websites, Pop-ups and Adverts

Adverts and pop-ups tend to plague some web sites. This is because many web sites are free, and they need to generate revenue with adverts; a bit like any commercial TV or radio channel. Most of the time, the adverts are innocuous, however some sites are a little more sinister and launch dozens of adverts, sometimes of an inappropriate nature.

Modern day machines and browsers do their best to stop this from happening, but they can't stop everything. There are some simple rules to help:

a) If a website appears that you didn't click or don't want, then close it immediately (there is no time limit so do not worry) - believe me when I say you are not their 1,000,000th visitor!

b) If the website keeps coming back, then reboot your computer. If it continues to come back, run an Anti-Virus scan.

c) Sometimes illegitimate companies will position themselves as genuine on Google or BING to trick people into looking at their site. Normally, the worst that will happen is you'll receive lots of annoying adverts which are difficult to close. Rebooting your machine should stop that - just remember not to go back to that site.

d) As we've seen from email scams, it is possible to get a virus or have money extorted by accessing unknown attachments. The same applies to accessing attachments (or downloads) from web sites. If a site tries to make you download or run a program you don't recognise, then close the web site or reboot your machine. **Do not run any program you didn't ask for**.

e) A good idea is to use your browser's 'Favourites' or 'Bookmarks' option - this is where you can store all your regular and trusted websites. If in doubt, use the 'Favourite' link to access a site, instead of the link you've been emailed or texted.

f) Be careful how you type a website address, or find a website in your search engine. Some devious people create websites with slightly altered names, for example by changing an 'l' to a '1' or missing off a letter. Their intention is to direct you away from the legitimate website you intended to access, to their illegitimate website. Often these websites are plagued with adverts and sometimes things more sinister.

6.3 Email Safety

We've already covered email scams, phishing and viruses, but there are other aspects to staying safe when using email.

Should you pay for goods or services over email?

The simple answer is: NO!

But what is safe to email and not safe to email? The same question can be applied to what information is safe to say over the phone.

Would you give your credit card details (long number, expiry date and the numbers on the back) to just anyone on the phone? No, you would probably want to check they are who they say they are.

The same applies to emailing your credit or debit card details. Think about what the receiver of the details can do with the information. If someone has your payment details, your name and address, they can buy anything they want.

There are lots of ways to pay for things online, email is not recommended - who knows where that email could end up? It is safer to pay for goods using a secure (padlocked) website, than over email.

Protecting your email address and password

We've already covered protecting the privacy of your email address, and not responding to phishing emails, SPAM or strange attachments.

Something we'll discuss in more detail later is ensuring the password on your email account is kept safe. Another option we'll discuss later is 'Multi-factor Authentication', or linking your email to your mobile phone.

6.4 Social Media safety and Cyber Bullying

Just like every*thing* is online, it seems that now every*one* is online too. Facebook, Twitter, Instagram have millions of subscribers, and can be excellent ways to stay in touch with friends and family. Unfortunately, as in life, there are unsavoury characters lurking.

Be careful what you share on Social media. It might be nice advertising your birthday to get those 'Best Wishes' messages or making everyone jealous by posting those holiday snaps, but remember other people might be able to see this.

Why is this a problem?

A couple of reasons:

a) If someone has your birthday and Mother's maiden name (very easy to trace in today's digital age), they can masquerade themselves as you. Possibly to your bank or utility provider. What are the first questions you're asked to validate your identity on the phone? How many of these details are on your social media account?

b) If someone knows your house is empty, they may want to see what you've left behind.

c) The more you post, the more someone can learn about you, e.g. your likes and dislikes, the places you visit, etc. This information can be used for what is known as 'social engineering' - this complex term means someone can use information about you to gain your trust. For example, if you post online that you went to a restaurant, someone could see your message and call you claiming to be the owner of that restaurant. Perhaps they'll say there was a problem with your credit card payment and ask you to repeat your details to them?

What can you do?

a) Check your privacy settings on sites like Facebook. You can alter who you share your holiday pictures or birthday with. For example, make sure your privacy settings are not set to Public, otherwise anyone can see this information.

b) Keep an eye on these privacy settings - some social media companies adjust their policies from time to time and reset them.

c) Think before you share or post something about yourself online.

d) Assume that if you post something on social media, someone, somewhere will see it.

e) Be wary of strange requests from people you don't know. If you don't know them, why would you want to connect with them? Even if they claim to know you, check their profile first. Don't rely on a mutual friend knowing them - do your own research. Criminals want to connect to your social media to see what you're up to, or when you're out - do not accept, even if you're curious.

f) Be wary of a request from someone you are already connected to on social media. Sometimes, social media accounts are cloned to manifest as someone you already know and trust. Ask yourself: "If I'm already connected to this person, why are they sending me a new request?" Call or email them to confirm. They may have been hacked.

Trolling and Cyber Bullying

When you post something on social media, ask yourself if you want the world to see it. It might be for security reasons, as above. Or it might be that your opinion or message may last longer that you expect.

I was once told an excellent anecdote about poison pen letters. Let's go back 100 years. If you wanted to send someone a poison pen letter, you would need to get out your paper and quill, write the letter, seal and stamp it, then take it to the post office for delivery. Let's say that took an hour at best. That hour would give you time to think if you really wanted to send that letter.

These days, abuse and vitriol can be constructed and posted within seconds, leaving no time for consideration.

What many people don't realise is how long these messages can last. A poison pen latter written a hundred years ago would likely have decayed or been destroyed by now. In a hundred years, the poison pen letters online today will still be accessible.

Cyber-bullying is real and dangerous. If you think you're subject to online abuse or trolling, then Facebook, Twitter etc. have mechanisms to block the offender and report them - do not suffer in silence.

Intermediate

6.4.1 Who gives out the website padlocks? Certificates and Certificate Authorities

Anyone can setup a website, publish it and then advertise it on Google or Bing to attract visitors. How do you know the site is genuine and they are who they say they are? We've seen that websites with padlocks are safe, but what makes them safe?

For a website to receive a padlock (what is also known as a certificate), it needs to prove its identify and validity to a Certificate Authority. These authorities are established organisations that request proof of company ownership, identification, etc. from a website creator to prove they are genuine. A bit like how you must prove your identity when opening a bank account by providing photo ID and proof of address.

Some sites will provide fake certificate, or have expired certificates - these should appear in your browser as insecure sites, normally alongside a warning explaining that the site may not be genuine. My advice is: if you access a website with a certificate error, then close it and don't return to it.

Key Lessons

- You wouldn't walk into a random building that pro-claimed to represent your bank and hand them your money for depositing. You'd want to make sure it was your bank. Make sure the websites you give your money or details to are genuine by looking for the padlock symbol.
- If a web site starts behaving in a way you don't like or didn't expect, then close it or reboot your computer.

- It's incredibly rare (almost impossible if you're running the latest Anti-Virus and patches on your computer) to get a virus just by accessing a web site. However, if the website forces you to download a file or prompts you to 'Accept' something you didn't ask for then close it and re-boot your machine.
- On your social media accounts, check your privacy settings - make sure you're not advertising to the world what you're up to.

7 Servicing your computer

You have a car. You bought it 8 years ago. You've never had it serviced, you've never MOT'd it. You've driven 90,000 miles in it, but never changed the tyres, let alone the oil or the windscreen washer fluid. Would you feel safe driving it around the M25?

The same applies to computers - they need some TLC.

Basic

7.1 RIP XP

Windows XP is no more - if you have a computer running Windows XP, then seriously consider changing it. Computer's aren't cheap, but using an old, insecure computer might prove more expensive (financially or emotionally) if you get a virus and lose all those documents and pictures.

Microsoft has stopped supporting Windows XP. This means they will no longer answer helpdesk calls about it and they won't produce updates to protect it against viruses. Other companies have followed suit. For example, Skype will stop working on XP eventually, and the latest software won't install on it - it's time to change.

A good point was raised in our first Neighbourhood Watch workshop. Shouldn't Microsoft be obliged to keep supporting Windows XP? A lot of companies are 'trapped' running XP - they have invested millions of pounds on systems that use XP and it will cost them millions to upgrade them.

The problem is Microsoft (and it's not just limited to Microsoft - Apple, Google, etc. do the same) must cease supporting old software. They are a business and they're here to make lots of money. Looking after old, outdated software is not profitable, and it's also not good for you because you don't get to experience all the nice, new fun features.

Incidentally, during one of the cyberattacks in 2017, due to the nature of the affected organisation, Microsoft did provide a fix to the virus that was attacking XP machines as a good-will gesture. Could they have done more? Possibly. However, questions also need to be levied at the organisations still running XP. It's an open question and one that will rage on, I'm sure.

Let's go back the car analogy. If you buy a new car, it will likely come with a warranty. After it expires, you'll probably be able to get spare parts for a number of years after. However, after a while, you won't be able to get a new clutch if yours fails. The manufacturer has moved on to their new model. You're left scouring the second-hand market for parts - or you can buy a new car. The same applies to your computer hardware and software.

If you have a machine running something older than Windows XP, then it would be safer for everyone in a museum.

You can get a good, cheap new laptop running Windows 10 for as little as £200 these days. Or ask yourself whether you need a computer. Would a tablet (as cheap as £50) be as useful, if all you do is browse the Internet, send emails and use video chat?

7.2 Updates and Patching

We all get annoyed when our machine needs updating. It slows down, it takes ages to reboot - it's all such a bother. However, updates and patches to your computer software are very important. Think of it like vaccinating your computer. It's the same as us getting the flu jab. If we get the jab, we significantly reduce our chances of getting the flu. If we don't, we run the risk of catching it. We generally inoculate our children from catching measles - why shouldn't PCs be inoculated too?

Bad people (and some good ones called 'Ethical hackers') are always on the lookout for a way to target or exploit a computer's software. The bad ones do it to give you viruses; the good ones do it to find problems (also known as vulnerabilities) so they can be fixed before the bad guys find them.

When these problems are found, they are reported to the software company, who then write a piece of code called a 'Patch' - this is effectively an Elastoplast. As a piece of software ages, it needs more patches. If XP was a person, it would look like an Egyptian mummy. When a new piece of software is created, the slate is wiped clean and the cycle of looking for problems or vulnerabilities starts again. It's a constant battle of good vs evil.

Updates aren't limited to Windows. Lots of software, such as Adobe, Skype, etc. require updates. As do Macs, and phones and tablets.

The lesson: if your computer wants to patch or update itself, then let it do it. If it's not convenient, then postpone it and do it next time. If you ignore it for long enough, you might catch a cold.

7.3 Granting access to your computer

As we saw in the first few chapters, people will try and get access to your machine to extort money. They do this by asking to install software on your machine that enables remote control of your desktop. One example is a tool called 'Team Viewer'. This is an excellent piece of software, but is unfortunately used for accessing people's machine against their will.

Many software companies however do need access to your computer; for example, if you call their support hotline.

The simple advice is: only let someone on your computer if you know who they are and want them to. It's the same as deciding whether to let someone in your house.

Key Lessons

- Get rid of your XP machine. You may be attached to it, or can't afford to buy a new one, but it could prove costlier to keep it. If you do have XP and insist on keeping it, then I would advise against connecting it to the Internet or plugging in any USB drives to keep it safe.
- If your machine wants to update itself, let it - don't put it off.
- Do not let anyone access your computer who you don't trust.
- Learn to recognise how your computer behaves and acts. If strange prompts, or messages start appearing, and you think something is wrong, then follow your gut and assume something is wrong. Run Anti-Virus scans and updates. Get some help if you're worried.

8 PINs and passwords, on phones, tablets and PC

Our online world is full of passwords, PINs and codes that are very difficult to remember. It's not a good idea to use the same password for everything, but having a combination of 3, 4 or 5 that you cycle or alter slightly is a good compromise.

Easy to guess passwords like '123456', 'password', or even pet or street names are so easy to guess (known as cracking or hacking a password) - you might as well not have a password at all.

You need to create complex passwords, but this makes remembering them even harder. So, what do we do? We write them down. This isn't necessarily a bad thing; it depends where and how we write them.

Would you store your Bank card PIN code in the same wallet/purse as your Bank card?

Basic

8.1 Password best practice

Advice on the best type of passwords is ubiquitous. That's not to say it's not important. I will repeat what is already advised on almost every website or book written on computer security.

a) Passwords should be 8 characters in length as a minimum.
b) Passwords should have uppercase, lowercase, numbers and symbols, e.g. P4ssWord$ (incidentally, this is not a good password, as it's still too obvious)

c) Passwords should not be obvious or recognisable words. Even street or pet names aren't a good idea unless they're made 'complex'.

d) You should consider changing your passwords on a regular basis, or cycling them if you have a number of regular ones.

e) If your password becomes compromised, e.g. someone guesses it or finds it out, then change all accounts that use that password and don't use it anymore.

f) Configure a phone number or backup email account for your most regularly used services, e.g. shopping and email. This means if you forget your password, it can be emailed or texted to you. Backup email accounts and phone numbers can also be used to warn you if your account has been hacked.

g) If you get an email from a company saying your password has been reset or changed and it's not something you were expecting then assume there is a problem. Log onto your account or contact the company to confirm. Don't click any links you receive as part of the password reset email.

h) It's a hard ask, but try to use different passwords for each account - even I struggle with this! At the very least have a collection of passwords and use across various accounts. If one of those passwords is guessed, or hacked then never use it again - again, even I struggle with this as you will soon see...

8.2 A way to remember your passwords

So how do we remember all these passwords? I bet you have a little book where you write them all? Where is it? Next to your laptop or PC? If someone stole your laptop, would they steal that book too? If they did, they'd have access to all your accounts, possibly even bank accounts.

Writing passwords down is OK, but needs a little trick to make it secure.

One idea is to remember a key word - It needs to be fairly long, e.g. Banana

Now let's change Banana and add a 4 in place of the 'a's - B4n4n4 - this can be your master password.

For each main account you have, like your email, or Amazon shopping, for example, create a couple of symbols to make the password unique. For example:

I. Amazon - £$

II. Gmail - ()

III. Facebook - %%

The idea is to use the master word, 'B4n4n4' in combination with the symbols, either at the end, the middle or the beginning of the master word. In the example, we'll use them at the end.

This means your passwords are:

Service	Symbol	Your whole password is
Amazon	£$	B4n4n4£$
Gmail	()	B4n4n4()
Facebook	%%	B4n4n4%%

You would only write the first two columns in your notebook. As long as you remember the master word, you can prompt yourself using the notebook with the symbols written down.

Now, if someone found or stole your notebook with your passwords, all they would know is the last two symbols of your password. They wouldn't know they needed to add B4n4n4 in front of the symbols.

Please don't use the B4n4n4 example I've used above, it's only an example, and not secure as a master password. Choose your own and be creative!

Another common way people remember passwords is to have a Master Password file. This a spreadsheet or document where all your passwords are stored. The problem is, if someone gets access to this file, then they get all your passwords!

If you have such a 'Master Password' file, then the following tips can help protect it:

a) Put a password on the Master Password file - most modern word processing or spreadsheet software will allow you to do this. Do not use a basic text editor program like Notepad on Windows - you will not be able to secure a file like this as easy. **Make sure this password is complex and not written down anywhere else!**

b) Consider putting the passwords in a paint or imaging program. Modern computers allow for text to be searched, but not images.

c) Name the file something obscure, e.g. don't call it 'passwords.txt' - 'recipes' or 'record collection' are less obvious to someone looking for a password file

d) Store the password file somewhere obscure, e.g. not on your desktop or 'My Documents'

e) Consider using the technique above, e.g. just writing down the symbols or characters in the 'Master Password' file and remembering the master password.

Remember - your password is like the key to your house. If you have spares, or leave one under the door mat, you increase the chances of someone finding it. Exercise a combination of caution, common sense and what works for you.

8.3 PIN codes

PIN codes are like passwords, but easier to remember. This also means they're easier to guess. Generally speaking, mobile phones and tablets are protected with PINs. Here's some advice for looking after your PIN codes.

a) Don't use birthdays, house umbers or numbers that someone might be able to guess if they know you.

b) Always put a pin on your phone or tablet - the recommended length is 6 digits.
   - 4 digits give someone 10,000 possibilities to guess, whereas 6 digits gives 1,000,000. Ten thousand might seem like a lot, but if someone is able to guess a few digits based on your birthday, then they're almost there.
c) If you don't put a pin on your tablet or phone and it is lost or stolen, then someone might be able to get access to your email and start trying to reset your passwords.
d) It's hard to remember all these pins, so use a couple or reverse them, so you know it's one or the other, e.g.
   - 369369
   - 963963

8.4 What if your password is guessed or hacked?

The first question is: how might this happen? There are a number of reasons:

a) You had an easy to guess password like '123456'
b) Someone has seen you enter your password. For example, if they were watching you enter it on a train or in a public space.
c) A company who stored your passwords, e.g. an online service or social media account you use, has been hacked and your password has been stolen.

The final point is unfortunately a common occurrence - you may have read or heard about it in the news. When a company is hacked, its collection of customer passwords is stolen. These are then sold to the highest bidder. If your account is in the list of stolen passwords, it could be used to hack your other accounts.

If you hear that a company who you use has been hacked, it's advisable to change your passwords immediately.

What happens if some gets hold of my password and hacks my account?

If someone guesses your password, or hacks it, it may not be immediately obvious. If any shopping services are affected, you might see transactions on your bank account you don't recognise.

If your email is hacked, then your email contacts might see strange emails coming from your account.

Good companies like Microsoft, Apple, eBay, Amazon and Gmail, for example, will detect if someone iffy has been accessing your email - it happened to me.

Someone from Algeria had attempted to access one of my email accounts. However, the email provider recognised that I don't often travel to Algeria to access my email, suspended my account and notified me using a backup email account.

The first thing I did? Change the accounts using that password, and never use that one again. However, I forgot one account and didn't change the password, then it was hacked. The hackers didn't get in though. How? I had used something called 'Multi-Factor Authentication'.

8.5 What is Multi-Factor Authentication? Or linking your phone to your password?

Intermediate

Many services, like shopping or email, offer something called Multi-Factor Authentication - a complex sounding phrase. We'll use MFA from now on.

Basically, this relies on the mantra: Something you have, Something you know. It is designed to increase security on your accounts, making them harder to be hacked.

If you think about it, it's likely you already use this technique. You have a bank card, but no one can use it without your PIN code. If someone guessed your PIN or saw it, they'd need to be in possession of your card.

Some banks even provide you with a little gadget that can be used to secure your login to online banking software.

It is also possible to link your phone to your email account, so when you access your email (either every time, or when it's accessed on a new device), you will get a text asking you to confirm this is OK.

The phone is the 'Something you have'. The password is the 'Something you know'.

If someone guesses your password and tries to log into your email, they won't be able to access your account unless they also have your phone. The likelihood of someone having access to what you have, e.g. your phone, and what you know, e.g. your password, is very small.

It can be daunting setting up MFA and there are some important things to consider; for example, what if you don't have your phone to receive the text message to log into your account? However, if you have a master email account where all your main correspondence and password reset emails, etc. go, then I would spend some time researching, or asking for some help on, setting up MFA.

Like I said earlier, when I forgot to change my password after it has been guessed, MFA stopped someone getting into my account. One day, my phone buzzed and I had an alert asking if I would authorise someone connecting to my Facebook account - it clearly wasn't me and I was able to deny the request.

It just goes to show that even experienced IT people make mistakes. In this case MFA saved my blushes.

Key Lessons

- Use complex passwords. Yes, they are annoying to remember, but it's less annoying than finding someone has hacked your account and spent all your money.

- If you do need to write your passwords down, then do so securely. It's not a myth that people write their passwords on a Post-It and stick them on their monitors. Would you leave a spare key in your latch, or write your pin on your bank card?
- If your password is hacked or guessed, then change it and never use it again.
- If you store your passwords in a file on your computer, secure the file as best as possible by putting a password on it and obscuring it as much as possible.
- If you feel confident enough, consider setting up Multi-Factor Authentication (MFA) on your most critical services, e.g. email. MFA will not 100% guarantee safety (nothing is 100% safe) but it will make it very, very difficult for someone to access your account.

9 Backups, USB drives and What is the Cloud?

The amount of times I've heard: My computer has gone wrong and I've lost all my photos/files - can you get them back? and I say: Have you made a backup? Then I watch their face drop when they realise the answer is: 'No'.

You only don't back up once.

What does this mean? Basically, when you've lost everything because your computer's gone wrong, you'll be sure to back up in the future - at least I hope you do.

Basic

The golden rule is, if it's important, then back it up. You can do this to the cloud, using iCloud, Dropbox, Google Drive, etc. - some of these are free, some you have to pay for, e.g. when you need more space.

There are so many ways to back up your important files these days. Indeed, it's much easier than it used to when we had dozens of floppy disks or had complicated CD burning software.

As well as cheap and easy to use USB drives (more on these in a bit), we now have 'The Cloud'.

9.1 The Cloud

The joke in IT is: there's no such thing as 'The Cloud', it's just someone else's computer! This is true.

In fact, 'The Cloud' is simply the Internet and someone decided to re-brand it one day, a bit like when *Marathon* became *Snickers*.

The Cloud is a great place to back your files up to, but you have to be careful:

a) When something is uploaded to the Cloud, it's simply another computer, somewhere else. You need to be sure the other computer is as safe too.
b) If you can access your files on the Cloud, then so can someone else - IF THEY HAVE YOUR PASSWORD!
c) It's important to secure your Cloud backups that store your files and pictures are with a complex password (remember them?)
d) Multi-factor Authentication can also be configured to protect some Cloud backup services.
e) You might not know it, but your photos could be being copied to somewhere on the Cloud. A lot of phones enable this by default, or encourage you to do this through the Next, Next, I Accept, Finish trick.

Have you heard of the Celebrity Photo Shaming scams? This is because 'Celebs' were taking (let's say inappropriate) selfies on their phones. Their phones copied these pictures to the Cloud, but the Celebs didn't set a complex password. Hackers were able to guess the password and get access to their selfies - the rest is history.

9.2 USB Drives

Another option is a USB drive - this is a more manual process. Whereas backups to Cloud should happen automatically (if they're working OK), you'll have to copy the files on the USB disk yourself.

Also, don't forget that if someone steals the USB stick, they have your files. If the files are important, e.g. bank or financial records, then store the USB stick safely as you would paper files, like in a safe.

Also consider that if you back up your important data to a USB drive, it will likely be stored in a similar location to your PC. In the event fire, flood or theft, you may lose both your computer device and your backup. It can be a good idea to store important backups in alternative, trusted locations, like a family member's house.

Remember: Two copies are better than one! (if they are stored securely).

Intermediate

9.3 Encrypting USB Drives and your computer

If you use a USB drive and want to protect your data, you can consider encrypting the USB drive. This means placing a password on the USB Drive, so if they steal it, or if you lose it and someone finds it, they won't be able to access your data.

Likewise, some machines (including tablets and mobile phones) give you the ability to encrypt the disk so if someone steals your device, they won't be able to run software against it to siphon the data.

How is this done?

If a computer's disk isn't encrypted and is stolen, even though it might be protected by pin or a password (e.g. so the thief can't log on to it), it is still possible to use software to access the information from the disk. This might sound like high-level espionage, but it is actually quite simple.

If the disk is encrypted, the thief can't access the data using the software.

It is also possible to purchase USB drives with built in pin codes or encryption, a bit like a pin code on a briefcase. The USB drive won't work unless the PIN code is set.

The dangers of encrypting?

Sometimes the software used to recover information from a disk can be used for legitimate means. For example, if a computer fails, it is sometimes possible to recover the information if the disk is still OK. However, if you encrypt the disk and the computer fails, then the data is generally lost. If you encrypt your computer, make sure you have good, secure backups.

Key Lessons

- If it's important to you, back it up!
- The question I ask most is: 'If your computer caught fire right now and you lost all your files, what would you do?' If the answer is: 'I'd lose all my data and it would be a disaster', then back up your files.
- If you do back up to 'The Cloud', remember to ensure the Cloud service you are using has a complex password, and consider using Multi-Factor Authentication.
- If you back up to USB drive, then store it somewhere safe, or consider encrypting it. If someone gets that USB drive, they get your data.

10 And Finally

Like they said on *Crime Watch*: Don't have nightmares!

Computers can be scary and difficult to fathom, but they can be an amazing way of connecting with family and friends and researching new facts and ideas.

If you look after your computer, it will look after you.

10.1 Useful Websites

- https://ico.org.uk/for-the-public/online/
- https://www.getsafeonline.org/
- https://www.ourwatch.org.uk/
- https://www.cyberaware.gov.uk/
- https://www.citizensadvice.org.uk/

10.2 Ideas for the next edition:

- Computer devices in your home, e.g. IoT.
- Better ways to manage your SPAM.
- Identity fraud/theft.
- Password Managers.
- More on Multi-Factor Authentication.
- Ad and pop-up blocking.
- Securing your home Wi-Fi.
- ISP and Bank free security/anti-virus software, and web site filters for safe browsing.
- Dangers of internet browsers.
- Saving Passwords in your browser.
- Installation of Browser Add-Ins, and changes to your home page.
- Using public internet terminal or shared PCs.
- Using free "untrusted" Wi-Fi and hotspots.

- Sharing your Wi-Fi, unprotected access, could lead to criminal activity on your Internet connection, which you may be liable for.
- Explanation of Internet Data usage (not really security, protect against unwanted costs)
- What is the difference between my mobile phone data, SMS messages, MMS messages, Skypes and other data messaging.
- Why do I get charged when I put an emoji on my SMS message, and I get free SMS messages - because it converts to an MMS message, and you are now charged ~40p per MMS message - read the prompts when your phone warns you that the SMS will be converted to an MMS.
- When does my data allowance for my phone get used up, should I use Wi-Fi at home
- My phone asked me to do an update, but is has used all of my data allowance to download the update software? Wait until you have Wi-Fi and it will not affect your data allowance. Read the warning message.
- Why can I sometimes send SMS messages, but not WhatsApp messages - you have mobile "phone" signal but not Data signal, SMS messages are old legacy technology and use the phone/voice communication mechanism.
- Dangers of GPS enabled apps and sharing your location.
- Snapchat enabled the map feature, by default all your friends can see exactly where you are.
- Facebook and Apple phones also have GPS tracking applications, so you can Find a friend - this can be useful - but may have security implications - only enable it when you need it enabled.

Printed in Great Britain
by Amazon

17595967R00051

PACIFIC PROFILES

VOLUME 13
IJN Bombers, Transports, Flying Boats & Miscellaneous Types
South Pacific 1942-1944

MICHAEL JOHN CLARINGBOULD

Avonmore Books

Pacific Profiles Volume 13
IJN Bombers, Transports, Flying Boats & Miscellaneous Types
South Pacific 1942-1944

Michael John Claringbould

ISBN: 978-0-6457004-6-6

First published 2024 by Avonmore Books
Avonmore Books
PO Box 217
Kent Town
South Australia 5071
Australia

Phone: (61 8) 8431 9780
avonmorebooks.com.au

A catalogue record for this
book is available from the
National Library of Australia

Cover design & layout by Diane Bricknell

Front Cover: Some of the varied IJN colour schemes of the South Seas (top to bottom): Yokohama Ku H8K2 Emily flying boat, Mitsubishi G6M1-L gunship converted to transport in two-tone "China Scheme" (Profile 3), Nippon Airways Kawanishi H6K2-L Mavis flying boat named Makigumo (Cirrus Cloud) (Profile 62), No. 251 Ku Nakajima J1N1-s Irving night fighter and a No. 582 Ku D3A2 used to lead aircraft for missions from Buin throughout early 1943 (Profile 11).

Back Cover: A Kisarazu Ku Model 11 Betty heads for Henderson Field over Guadalcanal's mountainous spine for a late afternoon reconnaissance in September 1942.

Contents

The author leans against a G4M1 Betty propeller at the former Rabaul airfield of Vunakanau in 2006.

About the Author

Michael Claringbould – Author & Illustrator

Michael spent his formative years in Papua New Guinea in the 1960s, during which he became fascinated by the many WWII aircraft wrecks which lay around the country and also throughout the Solomon Islands. Michael subsequently served widely overseas as an Australian diplomat throughout Southeast Asia and the Pacific, including Fiji (1995-1998) and Papua New Guinea (2003-2005). Michael's history of the Tainan Naval Air Group in New Guinea, *Eagles of the Southern Sky*, received worldwide acclaim as the first English-language history of a Japanese fighter unit, and was subsequently translated into Japanese. An executive member of Pacific Air War History Associates, Michael holds a pilot license and PG4 paraglider rating. He continues to develop his skills as a digital aviation artist.

Other Books by the Author

A6M2/3 Zero-sen New Guinea and the Solomons 1942 (Osprey, 2023)

Black Sunday (Second Edition), 2022

Eagles of the Southern Sky (2012, with Luca Ruffato)

F4U Corsair versus Zero the Solomons 1943-44 (Osprey, 2022)

Nemoto's Travels The illustrated saga of a Japanese floatplane pilot in the first year of the Pacific War (2021)

Operation I-Go Yamamoto's Last Offensive – New Guinea and the Solomons April 1943 (2020)

Operation Ro-Go 1943 (Osprey, 2023)

P-39 / P-400 Airacobra versus A6M2/3 Zero-sen New Guinea 1942 (Osprey, 2018)

P-47D Thunderbolt versus Ki-43 Hayabusa New Guinea 1943/44 (Osprey, 2020)

Pacific Adversaries Volume One Japanese Army Air Force vs The Allies New Guinea 1942-1944 (2019)

Pacific Adversaries Volume Two Imperial Japanese Navy vs The Allies New Guinea & the Solomons 1942-1944 (2020)

Pacific Adversaries Volume Three Imperial Japanese Navy vs The Allies New Guinea & the Solomons 1942-1944 (2020)

Pacific Adversaries Volume Four Imperial Japanese Navy vs The Allies - The Solomons 1943-1944 (2021)

Pacific Profiles Volume One Japanese Army Fighters New Guinea & the Solomons 1942-1944 (2020)

Pacific Profiles Volume Two Japanese Army Bomber & Other Units, New Guinea and the Solomons 1942-44 (2020)

Pacific Profiles Volume Three Allied Medium Bombers, A20 Series, South West Pacific 1942-44 (2020)

Pacific Profiles Volume Four Allied Fighters: Vought F4U Corsair Series Solomons Theatre 1943-1944 (2021)

Pacific Profiles Volume Five Japanese Navy Zero Fighters (land-based) New Guinea and the Solomons 1942-1944 (2021)

Pacific Profiles Volume Six Allied Fighters: Bell P-39 & P-400 Airacobra South & Southwest Pacific 1942-1944 (2022)

Pacific Profiles Volume Seven Allied Transports: Douglas C-47 series South & Southwest Pacific 1942-1945 (2022)

Pacific Profiles Volume Eight IJN Floatplanes in the South Pacific 1942-1944 (2022)

Pacific Profiles Volume Nine Allied Fighters: P-38 series South & Southwest Pacific 1942-1944 (2022)

Pacific Profiles Volume 10: Allied Fighters: P-47D Thunderbolt series Southwest Pacific 1943-1945 (2023)

Pacific Profiles Volume 11: Allied Fighters: USAAF P-40 Warhawk series South and Southwest Pacific 1942-1945 (2023)

Pacific Profiles Volume 12: Allied Fighters: P-51 & F-6 Mustang series New Guinea and the Philippines 1944-1945 (2023)

South Pacific Air War Volume 1: The Fall of Rabaul December 1941–March 1942 (2017, with Peter Ingman)

South Pacific Air War Volume 2: The Struggle for Moresby March–April 1942 (2018, with Peter Ingman)

South Pacific Air War Volume 3: Coral Sea & Aftermath May-June 1942 (2019, with Peter Ingman)

South Pacific Air War Volume 4: Buna & Milne Bay June-September 1942 (2020, with Peter Ingman)

South Pacific Air War Volume 5: Crisis in Papua September-December 1942 (2022, with Peter Ingman)

Solomons Air War Volume 1 Guadalcanal August-September 1942 (2023, with Peter Ingman)

Solomons Air War Volume 2 Guadalcanal & Santa Cruz October 1942 (2023, with Peter Ingman)

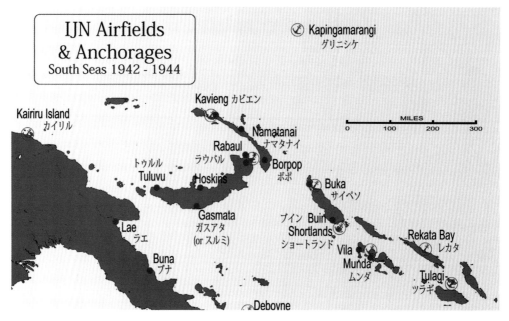

A map of the South Pacific theatre of operations (known as the South Seas theatre to the Japanese), showing airfields and seaplane anchorages used by the IJN throughout New Guinea and the Solomons.

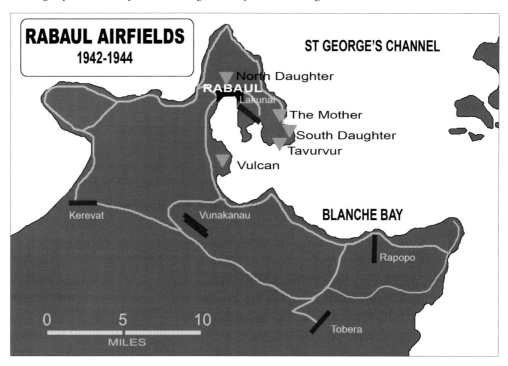

After occupying Rabaul in January 1942, the Japanese possessed two Australian-built airfields at Lakunai and Vunakanau both of which underwent much expansion during 1942-43. Located between an active volcano (Tavurvur) and the harbour Lakunai was mainly used as a fighter strip, while the more expansive Vunakanau became the main regional bomber base. Three other fighter strips at Kerevat, Rapopo and Tobera were constructed in 1943. Kerevat was mainly used for maintenance purposes.

Glossary and Abbreviations

Note: Japanese terms are in italics. Japanese names are presented with the surname first as per Japanese convention. Allied code names for Japanese planes are used because they are widely recognised.

Buntai	Equivalent to a *chutai*, but normally having an administrative or command status.
Buntaicho	Leader of a *buntai*.
Chutai	An aircraft formation which normally comprised a strength of nine aircraft. IJN fighter and bomber units normally had between three to five *chutai* with a headquarters detachment.
Chutaicho	A Japanese flight leader of officer rank who commands a *chutai*.
Daitai	An administrative or operational term denoting a collection of typically two or three *chutai*. Hence a *kokutai* might be divided into two *daitai*. This was a pre-war IJN term although some units continued to use it as late as 1943.
FCPO	Flying Chief Petty Officer (IJN).
Flyer1c	Aviator first class (IJN).
FPO1c	Flying Petty Officer first class (IJN).
FPO2c	Flying Petty Officer second class (IJN).
Hikotaicho	Operational commander of a *kokutai*, one rank under a *hikocho*.
Hikocho	Administrative and overall commander of a *kokutai*, superior in rank to a *hikotaicho*.
Hinomaru	The red disc on the Japanese flag representing the sun and also used as a roundel on Japanese aircraft.
Hokoku	Inscriptions (translating as "patriotic") which signified that an aircraft was donated by an individual, organisation or corporation.
IJN	Imperial Japanese Navy.
JAAF	Japanese Army Air Force.
Kanji	Adopted Chinese characters used as part of Japanese writing. In the case of the IJN, they were used alongside *katakana*. IJN wartime script uses many characters no longer recognisable in modern Japanese. All Japanese crew lists had their names written in *kanji*.
Katakana	Phonetic characters used in written Japanese, usually used for geographic place names.
Kokutai	An IJN air group, consisting of between three to six *chutai*.
Ku	abbreviation of *kokutai*.
Lieutenant (jg)	Lieutenant (junior grade).
MN	Manufacturer's Number.
NMF	Natural Metal Finish.
Romanji	Roman (Western) letters.
Shotai	A Japanese term defining an IJN flight, usually of three aircraft, however later in the theatre such flights often comprised four aircraft, especially within No. 204 *Ku*.
Shotaicho	Flight leader of a *shotai*.
USAAF	United States Army Air Force.
USN	United States Navy.

Introduction

Welcome to the markings of IJN land-based units which served in the South Seas. Importantly, note that this volume excludes floatplane and Zero units, as both are covered separately in *Volumes Five* and *Eight* of this *Pacific Profiles* series. Included are bombers, transports and flying boats along with a handful of more esoteric types such as Irving night fighters and reconnaissance and dive-bomber Judys. Several aircraft and IJN units are covered for the first time, such as one of the pair of Yokosuka Naval Technical Department Bettys which visited Rabaul in April 1942 to undertake technical research (see Profile 69). Other rare units to receive coverage for the first time include No. 151 *Ku*, a dedicated reconnaissance unit; and Val *kokutai* Nos. 965, 552, 31 and 701 *Ku*, the last of which operated Nells later in the war.

The *Pacific Profiles* series covers only South Seas IJN units as, in the opinion of this author at least, this theatre was the key one in which the future of Japan's struggles occurred. All of these *kokutai* at some stage operated from Rabaul. At times some units based in the Central Pacific also strayed into Rabaul and the Solomons, or at least their aircraft did. These are covered too.

I was emboldened to explore IJN markings more broadly when it became clear that no accurate profile existed of the most famous Betty of all; the bomber in which Admiral Yamamoto Isoroku, commander of the Combined Fleet, was shot down over Bougainville on 18 April 1943. This Betty was administratively assigned to No. 705 *Ku*'s No. 5 *Buntai*, and as such had a narrow white split stripe across the fin, confirmed by post-war photos taken at the site (see Profile 82), a key detail omitted to date. Other renditions incorrectly illustrate a tail prefix, which was painted out for security reasons. Most paintings of the bomber are also inaccurate, the most glaring of which portrays Yamamoto's bomber in the pre-war two-tone "China Scheme" camouflage! The Mitsubishi manufacturer's number (known since the 1960s), indicates it was a new overall green Model 11 with a truncated tail, having been delivered to Rabaul only a few weeks before its demise. Even the name of Yamamoto's pilot is published incorrectly in Western histories which state his name as Kotani Takeo (or vice-versa depending on surname order), whose rank varies according to each publication. In fact, the relevant aviator was FCPO Kotani Takashi (小谷立), whose first name was Takashi, not Takeo, as hand-written in the unit's operations log. With such fundamental errors being repeated in Western histories, imagine the errors which lurk elsewhere pertaining to more esoteric IJN markings and history.

IJN Markings

The markings of Imperial Japanese Navy aircraft, whilst complex, nonetheless conformed to strict methodology. The Japanese fondness for order and numbers is inherent in these systems. The key to understanding them revolves around their placement in the Combined Fleet and Department of Navy's operational and administrative structures, alongside commensurate Orders of Battle. Further guidance is offered by breakdowns within the units themselves, and the numerous markings edicts and directives which were promulgated and revised throughout the conflict. Disturbing this order however are the incessant restructuring of these ORBATs, along with regular changes to tail prefixes, some of which are not documented. The Combined Fleet underwent three restructures in 1942 alone: the first in April 1942, then in July (mainly carrier units) before culminating in the major administrative reconfiguration of October/November 1942.

As to the *kokutai* themselves, some continued internal legacy structures they had adopted in the China theatre, not discarding them until 1943. Others overlaid administrative structures upon their operational markings, No. 705 *Ku* being an exemplar of this idiosyncrasy which produces no end of complication and seeming contradiction. The colour and structure of unit tail codes was determined at Fleet (*kantai*) level. Nevertheless, sometimes the unit prefix was not applied or was painted out due to security concerns. This occurred often at Rabaul which was rightly considered a frontline base from late 1942 onwards. The style and application of unit prefixes was made at *kokutai* level, authorised by the commanding officer. Here, there is no shortage of differing styles, from hand-painted to stencilled, some with eccentric serifs, with or without accentuating piping.

The first 1942 IJN reorganisation of April followed the concluding phase of Japanese conquests from Malaya to New Guinea. A key component of this restructure was the fact that the 11th Air Fleet was transformed from an umbrella organisation for land-attack units into the *de facto* South Seas land-based air force, headquartered at Rabaul. Henceforth it was charged with protecting the vast geographic expanse of New Guinea and the Solomons. Note that the Japanese regarded this area as one theatre, the South Seas (*Nanto Homen)*, whilst the Allies split it into two – the South West Pacific Area and the South Pacific Area.

On the other hand, Netherlands East Indies-based units fell under the Southwest Area Fleet (*Nansei Homen*), some of which also showed up at Rabaul for temporary or extended duty. Guilty units include the Kanoya *Ku*, Takao *Ku* and No. 3 *Ku*. When the Takao *Ku* sent a major contingent to Rabaul in September 1942, it sported red tail codes, but surprisingly not Kanoya *Ku* which ironically was ordered to have red tail codes but felt compelled to have white ones to conform to the rest of the 11th Air Fleet. Both this latter unit and its parent 21st Air Flotilla were reassigned to the 11th Air Fleet on 15 April 1943. The Takao *Ku* remained under the umbrella of the 23rd Air Flotilla during its short deployment to Rabaul, which remained based in the Southwest Area until transferred to the 13th Air Fleet on 20 September 1943.

Another IJN reorganisation soon followed in 1942 when on 14 July Combined Fleet reorganised its carrier units as a result of the Midway disaster. Unfortunately several key documents pertaining to the markings for the second restructure have yet to surface. Primary sources provide listings of unit prefixes and associated units; however these fail to align colour associations for the land-based units. This is relevant as markings of some carrier units *per se* also affect this volume, as an eclectic assortment of ex-carrier airframes wound up serving Rabaul's land-based units. Primary source documentation for colours for the tail codes of the First, Second and Third Southern Expeditionary Fleets in particular are incomplete. Whilst several unit codes are ordained as red, other key unit colours are undefined. The relevant Combined Fleet orders will surely exist somewhere for the 14 July restructure, either in original format or translated by Allied Intelligence, however they have thus far eluded researchers. Nonetheless, adequate photographic evidence gives us confidence that all 11th Air Fleet units used white or black tail codes.

The October/November 1942 IJN Restructure

Now we turn to the most far-reaching and impactful IJN restructure of all – that which took place in October/November 1942. It is important to note that the first two 1942 restructures were implemented by Combined Fleet *per se* whereas this one was decreed instead by Air Headquarters within the Ministry of Navy (*Koku Honbu*). This was the major restructure of the war, and it thus requires attention to detail. Indeed, it still causes confusion today, as we will see.

This rearrangement was instigated by Tokyo bureaucrats on security grounds, and arises from the Japanese enthusiasm for order and numbers. When Japanese forces first swept through Malaya and expanded southwards, the Japanese military boasted about both the origins of their units and their associations via Japanese media. However, following the setbacks of mid-1942, especially at Midway, the Japanese military embarked on a plan to obviscate these origins. Accordingly, the Ministry of Navy drew up a stratagem whereby all land-based air units were redesignated according to the sequential numbering scheme outlined below. Its introduction was foreshadowed in October 1942 when No. 14, Toko and Kanoya *Ku* were redesignated as Nos. 802, 851 and 751 *Ku* respectively (note, not the 802nd, 851st and 751st *Ku* which are the invention of the Western mindset, and undermine the purpose of the system).

The system is logical to decipher. The first digit determines the unit's aircraft type, the second denoted the original base, whilst the third identified the sequential allocation, i.e. the first, second etc unit operating the same aircraft type from the same base.

Aircraft Type	Original Base	Sequential Number
1 - reconnaissance	0, 1, 2 – Yokosuka District	1, 2, 3 etc
2 – fighter	3, 4 – Kure District	
5 – dive bomber	5,6,7–Kanoya/ Sasebo Districts	
7 – land attack bomber	8,9–Maizuru District	
8 – seaplane		
9 – Fleet support		
10 – Fleet transport		

Thus, by way of example, the Kanoya *Ku* which operated land-attack bombers ("7"), originally from Kanoya/Sasebo ("5"), was the first bomber unit to originate from that district ("1"), thus becoming No. 751 *Ku*. It is equally practical to work backwards, for example No. 802 *Ku* indicates it was operating seaplanes ("8") and was the second such seaplane unit to originate from the Yokosuka District ("0"). This representative system applied to all land-based *kokutai* throughout the IJN.

To complicate matters, this essentially administrative restructure was attended by widespread personnel and unit movements and replacements. For example, the most significant bomber unit to operate in the theatre, No. 4 *Ku*, departed as a result of this restructure, to later return to the South Seas in the form of No. 702 *Ku*. This system also explains the larger unit numbers such as the first specialist transport unit No. 1001 *Ku*, the first Combined Fleet transport unit ("10") from Yokosuka ("0").

Note that assimilation and exchange of airframes within the 11th Air Fleet often challenges the decoding of markings. An obfuscating exemplar in the South Seas was the Vals of No. 2 *Ku*, which became No. 582 *Ku* in the late 1942 restructure. In December 1942 this *kokutai* absorbed a full chutai of No. 956 *Ku* (which had been No. 40 *Ku* prior to the October/November IJN restructure). This detached *chutai* arrived at Rabaul on 10 November 1942 with ten Vals, however it initially continued to operate under the umbrella of the Singapore-based Second Southern Expeditionary Fleet. The detachment was subsequently absorbed by No. 582 *Ku* around 24 November, however this move fails to appear in any IJN Order of Battle, perhaps as it was considered piecemeal logistics. The integrated *chutai* continued to operate administratively within No. 582 *Ku* as its own distinct *buntai* after its assimilation. To add to the mix when operating from Bougainville, No. 582 *Ku* also absorbed a collective of Vals from the carrier *Hiyo* after they were dispossessed from their damaged ship. The convoluted expliqué is outlined in Chapter 3 encompassing No. 2/582 *Ku*, a sobering case study of conformity going haywire, but conformity nonetheless.

Note also that whilst Allied air forces were generally in the habit of issuing directives to be implemented in the field, the Japanese system was more often the reverse. The 11th Air Fleet in particular saw its initiatives reissued as formal orders cut by Tokyo simply to formalise existing practices at Rabaul, a base never short of field initiative.

Hokoku Markings (報国) - Patriotic Presentation Airframes

From the outset of Japan's hostilities with China, both the IJN and JAAF encouraged patriotic civilians and organisations to raise funds to underwrite aircraft production. Donors were rewarded by having their names stencilled on the fuselage. These donors ranged far and wide across the empire; not only from within Japan itself, donations also sprang forth from Taiwan, Korea and even as far as Mongolia (see Profile 83). There was no standardised system for raising and donating funds for such. Wealthy individuals seized the opportunity to make individual donations which enhanced their social prestige. Companies took up collections among their employees, and there were also "All Japan" initiatives which entailed country wide patriotic appeals.

Japan's major newspaper *Asahi Shimbun* along with other newspapers and magazines sponsored the *hokoku* initiative. These publications advertised the launch of campaigns and subsequently publicised names of individuals and identified the highest contributors to appeals. A case in point is the "All Japan Schoolgirls" series which raised funds from the mobilisation of school students across the nation. Monies were donated by students, teachers, families and the wider community. Collectors could be seen parading along Japan's streets soliciting contributions from passers-by.

Furthermore, there was considerable fanfare and ceremony when donated aircraft were "presented" to the nation, during which relevant airframes were formally dedicated and blessed in well attended functions. These ceremonies included line-ups at airfields including Tokyo's Haneda airport where the donated airframes were paraded in a show of patriotism along with much fanfare. Presentations were also made in public halls or shrines such as the Kyoritsu Auditorium, Tokyo, or the Mengjiang Shrine in Hebei Province (see Profiles 83 and 86).

Hinomaru Styles

The reasons behind the various formats of the *hinomaru*, including the white square background more commonly seen on Bettys, have been misrepresented over the years. The first modifications to the standard *hinomaru* stem from a Department of Navy order dated 21 August 1942, proscribing either a 75mm white outline or a white square extending 75mm from the edge of the *hinomaru* equidistant from the centre. This was to be applied in the factory to all fuselage *hinomaru* regardless of aircraft colour. Curiously, photographic evidence demonstrates that *hinomarus* with white piping were already being applied to camouflaged backgrounds prior to August 1942.

Mitsubishi favoured the white square option for their Betty production run, whilst Aichi applied a similar white square to initial production runs of D3A2 Vals. This initial Navy edict was followed by a variation dated 5 October 1942 which altered the width dimensions. The initial Department of Navy order dated 21 August 1942 instructed:

A. Wings and fuselages to both be marked with *hinomaru*.

B. Those *hinomaru* applied to the fuselage of camouflaged airplanes will be accentuated with either a white square or white piping.

C. The inner half of the wing leading edge will be painted yellow for camouflaged aircraft.

The width of the white piping sometimes tended to be thinner than the 75mm mandated in the subsequent 5 October 1942 instructions. Painting out the white backgrounds, both squares and piping, was widely implemented by Rabaul's units as the war progressed as it was judged by relevant commanders that the white highlighted the aircraft's visibility. There was, in particular, a widespread practice at Rabaul of erasing the white square background which appeared on Vals arriving from the factory, although a handful were left alone, at least shortly after delivery. No formal orders were issued by either the Combined Fleet or Tokyo to erase these white backgrounds. Rabaul took the initiative on the matter, however for some reason white square backgrounds on the Bettys were left extant; at least no photo has turned up with one expunged. The above cited markings order explains why the fuselage *hinomaru* on IJN airframes appeared in three formats: initially the *hinomaru* by itself, then some with white piping or white square, and finally the above formats with the white painted over.

Note that in the illustrations the yellow leading edge has often been omitted. This is not because it wasn't there, but rather its dimensions varied on each different airframe.

Tailplane lines - 編流測定線

The red or white lines which mostly appear on Val (and carrier Kate) tailplanes have been misinterpreted in Western publications as guides to assist sighting of the rear gun azimuth. Instead, their real purpose was to serve as a visual navigation aid from which the observer/ gunner could calculate drift-angles. Furthermore, the lines were applied in the field during operational service, not in the factory. This explains the considerable variation in both the number of lines and their spacing. Some lines were shortened, extending only briefly from leading edges, whilst others were cut short at the elevators. Usually between four to six lines were applied to each stabiliser, normally spaced in five-degree intervals.

The lines were projected from the nominated fuselage observation point, so that the rear-seater could sight along them from the epicentre. A circular manual drift computer could then be consulted to calculate the aircraft's drift rate. This pre-war technique was also used initially by Allied air forces and fleet air arms, but only early on. Typically, American aviator legend Charles Lindbergh used the concept to assist his pre-war distance flights. Drift lines were apparent on the horizontal stabiliser of his Lockheed Sirius floatplane when he staged through Japan in late 1931. The Japanese technical term for these lines in *kanji* is 編流測定線 "Delineated Measurement Lines".

Summary

The above appears complicated, because unfortunately it is. Whilst national and unit markings rules are clear cut, they were mixed up by numerous restructures, modifications to orders and field initiatives including obviscation of prefixes. Added to this were inventory swaps and crossovers of administrative and operational structures. When airframes were transferred to other units, the heat of battle meant that markings adjustments took time to implement. Thus, we see that an aircraft's markings were defined by the timeframe in which it served, the technical orders which applied to its national insignia, subsequent field initiatives and the mixing of inventories. There remain unfortunately limited gaps in our understanding of how this all played out, including the scheme of the Ki-46s deployed by the IJN as a night fighter later in the war. I hope this volume advances the understanding of the markings of these fascinating aircraft.

Michael John Claringbould
Canberra, Australia
December 2023

CHAPTER 1
Technical Notes

Technical and operating data for IJN aircraft types are readily available elsewhere, and there is little point in repeating any of this. Nonetheless, air operations in the South Seas portended numerous and unique eccentricities due to the tropical conditions and isolation, the more pertinent of which relating to the Val, Judy and Betty are highlighted below. Further technical information is related via the diagrams at the end of this chapter.

Val

The dive-bomber of choice for Rabaul's land-based units was both the Aichi D3A1 and D3A2 Val. The D3A2's more powerful engine enabled it to climb faster than its predecessor and to cruise about twenty knots faster too. Nonetheless both models were limited to two fixed forward-firing 7.7mm machine guns, and a single flexible 7.7mm machine gun on a swing mount fixed in the rear observer compartment. At Rabaul some units field-modified the airframe by replacing the rear 7.7mm machine gun with a 20mm machine-canon.

Whilst suitable for shipping attacks, particularly when armed with a 250-kilogram bomb, the bomb load dictated the range in a theatre where distance ruled. At the extreme end of capacity, Vals were able to tote one 250-kilogram and two 60-kilogram bombs each. They had the ability of toting a hefty fuselage drop-tank too, increasing their range but limiting the bomb load to two 60-kilogram bombs. Their destructive power was relatively small, and only a providential hit could hope to inflict significant damage on a ship. When operating from Buin, Vals were able to routinely tote a 250-kilogram bomb plus one or two 60-kilogram bombs during the central Solomons campaign, as New Georgia targets involved only a 300-mile return trip. Nonetheless, in their final month of operations from Rabaul, Allied fighters swarmed over almost every Val mission, as evidenced by this VMF-212 report of 15 Feb 1944, whose Corsairs covered the US Marine landing at Green Island:

> The Vals came in, in three sections of two each. They seemed to fire with the first good burst that went into them. Evasive actions were ineffective. Fire from the rear gunner did not bother any of the fighters. In short, it was an ice-cream festival after battling Zeros over Rabaul.

Judy

The Aichi D4Y1 Judy was adopted into IJN service type on 1 July 1942 with the service designation Type 2 carrier reconnaissance plane. Following production modification which commenced in October 1942 to the D4Y1 *Suisei* Model 11, later in 1943 it was redesignated as a carrier dive bomber. The first deliveries to Rabaul occurred in February 1943 when two reconnaissance versions were sent to No. 253 *Ku*, and two more to the carrier *Shokaku*. No. 501 *Ku* was the first Judy unit to use the type in action as a dive bomber. Its eclectic deployment saw them drop bombs against the US carriers which raided against Rabaul in early November 1943, the type often misidentified by USN pilots during these occasions as the JAAF Ki-61 Tony. Note that the subsequent model, the D4Y2 Model 12, had a more powerful engine installed however it did not enter production until May 1944 and thus saw no service in the South Seas theatre.

Betty

The backbone of the IJN strike force at Rabaul was the Mitsubishi G4M1 Betty medium bomber. By early 1944 dozens of Betty air and ground crew had been captured, providing the Allies with meticulous detail on the bomber's performance and shortcomings. Although it had impressive range, calamitous losses during the first two months of the Guadalcanal campaign forced future bombing missions to higher levels, thus reducing bombing accuracy. Cruising at altitudes up to 9,000 metres (nearly 30,000 feet) required electrically-heated suits worn by crews. Similarly climbs to high altitudes required oxygen. The aircraft commander usually opened the master oxygen valve around 4,000 metres, however there was only sufficient supply for about four hours, so consumption was carefully monitored.

The large Betty had several idiosyncrasies. Following prolonged flights, its carburettors often fell out of adjustment causing incorrect fuel/air ratios. Brake pads quickly wore out on the heavy bomber too, and so did the maingear tyres made by the Fujikura or Meiji Tyre companies. Betty engines required overhaul every 300 hours, but combat demands often extended this to 500.

New Bettys from the Mitsubishi factory were first delivered to the trial airfield at Suzuka in Japan, where crews arrived from Rabaul or Tinian to collect them. The Betty's centre of gravity moved too far forward when not carrying ordnance, so at Rabaul five or six 60-kilogram sandbags were loaded into the rear fuselage to correct this. The airframe vibrated considerably during both taxiing and flight, which unsettled new pilots. A key point is that all Betty undersurfaces on all models were NMF, not grey as is often misrepresented.

Tail gunners had the worst of it as Allied fighter pilots preferred to attack the Betty from the rear, and records show this crewmember was the most frequently wounded in combat. Early model G4M1s with the full tail cone had the azimuth of the rear 20mm gun restricted by the enclosed housing. This culminated in No. 751 *Ku* initiating the first crude field modification to the birdcage housing at Kavieng in early 1943, whereby the rear half of the cone was severed thus permitting a greater field of fire. This modification actually reduced the bomber's speed by three knots, however Mitsubishi later produced a factory modification, the first truncated models of which arrived at Rabaul from Tinian in August 1943. The rear tail cone was again modified subsequently on the last batches of G4M1s, and also featured on the G4M2. This streamlined "clam shell" design split open when required.

Whilst the standard crew compliment was seven, reconnaissance mission Bettys often carried an extra photographer, and command aircraft usually bore an extra officer resulting in crews of eight or even nine. These numbers dropped considerably due to later crew shortages, and by the end of 1943 missions were being routinely flown with just five or six crew. The bomber's Achilles' heel was a lack of self-sealing petrol tanks and no protective crew armour. The Betty ditched cleanly, however, and was designed to stay afloat. There were numerous cases where downed crews survived significant durations in Pacific seas.

The bomber's standard bomb load was a dozen 60-kilogram or two 250-kilogram bombs (or mixtures thereof) which, unless placed squarely on target, usually had limited effect. No Betty crew ever wore parachutes, thus incurring higher crew losses than warranted. However, a key point is that the exit points for the bomber under duress were small and limited, rendering it near-impossible to evacuate in flight. The bomber's power/weight ratio saw sluggish take-off performance, thus confining operations to principal airfields, mainly Kavieng, Buka and Rabaul (Vunakanau). The bomber's heavy weight resulted in another key consideration, being that most serious accidents were due to landing gear collapse. Other satellite fields such as Ballale and Buin were used by the G4M1 for emergency landings, refuelling or as a temporary base from which to conduct reconnaissance missions.

A final but seminal point about deployment of the Betty in the South Seas is that the G4M2 Model did see service at Rabaul, albeit brief, a fact not acknowledged until this publication. This fact is verified from no less than seven separate ground crew interrogations by Allied intelligence following the sinking of *Kowa Maru* on 20 February 1944. Not only did they describe the square windows, revolving turret and H6 radar installation, one engineer even provided considerable technical detail on the water injection systems in the upgraded *Kasei* engines. The first four G4M2s, which were assigned to No. 751 *Ku*, arrived from Truk in January 1944 for trials at Rabaul in night operations. Further examples arrived the following month. These airframes were equipped with the H6 radar and were a completely different airframe to the G4M1 (per Profile 113). This fact has escaped historians to date as Allied low-level photos of them at Vunakanau do not exist, or if they do, have yet to surface.

Figure 1 – GM41/2 Betty markings and variants

This sequential series highlights the intricate markings and airframe changes to the mainstay of the IJN strike force – the G4M1 Betty - as the war progressed. These timeframes specifically apply to the South Seas theatre, omitting the more complex markings and airframe changes which occurred during the last phase of the war in the Philippines and closer to Japan itself. Note also that the appearance of certain Betty models at Rabaul sometimes lagged well behind when they left the factory.

The first production G4M1 was adopted for service by the IJN on 2 April 1941 and designated the Land Attack Bomber Model 11. Fitted initially with the Kasei 11 engine, from August 1942 onwards airframes left the factory with the upgraded Kasei 15 fitted with a larger supercharger. Individual exhaust stacks were applied to production runs from September 1943 onwards. The G4M2 installed Kasei 21 engines with methanol-water injection. This upgraded airframe came installed with a four-bladed propeller and hydraulic constant-speed governor, replacing the previous three-bladed unit. The power-operated dorsal turret with twin 20mm canons increased the aircraft's weight considerably to 12,500 kilograms from 9,498 kilograms. Whilst the first production G4M2 left the Mitsubishi factory July 1943, the type did not appear in the South Seas theatre until early 1944.

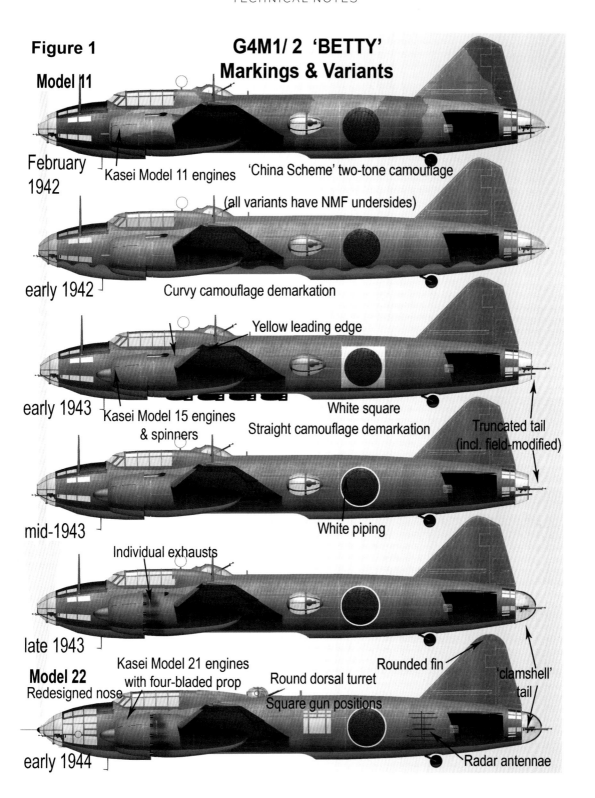

Figure 1

G4M1/ 2 'BETTY'
Markings & Variants

Model 11

February 1942

Kasei Model 11 engines

'China Scheme' two-tone camouflage

(all variants have NMF undersides)

early 1942

Curvy camouflage demarkation

Yellow leading edge

early 1943

Kasei Model 15 engines & spinners

White square

Straight camouflage demarkation

Truncated tail (incl. field-modified)

mid-1943

White piping

Individual exhausts

late 1943

Model 22

Redesigned nose

Kasei Model 21 engines with four-bladed prop

Round dorsal turret

Square gun positions

Rounded fin

'clamshell' tail

early 1944

Radar antennae

Figure 2

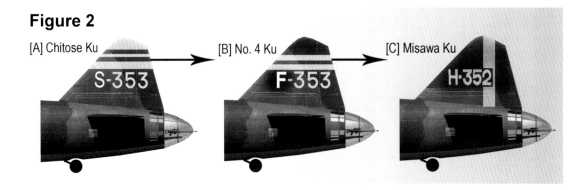

[A] Chitose Ku   S-353   [B] No. 4 Ku   F-353   [C] Misawa Ku   H-352

Figure 2

Model 11 Betty MN 1365 ditched in shallow water in the Solomons on 10 September 1942, after which it was salvaged and studied extensively by Allied intelligence. The tail of this early model green and brown "China Scheme" bomber provides a text-book example of the numerous unit markings changes caused by inventory changes. The bomber first served with the Chitose *Ku* as S-353 (A) before it was later transferred to the No. 3 *Buntai* of No. 4 *Ku* in late February 1942 (B), where it became F-353 with two fin stripes. In early September 1942 it was reassigned to the Misawa *Ku* No. 3 *Buntai* and renumbered H-352 (C). This aircraft is also illustrated in Profile 77. The photo of the tail of this salvaged bomber (see below) shows traces of all three schemes.

Figure 3 - MARKINGS

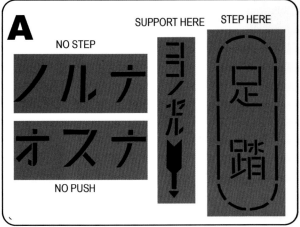

B TAIL CODES

-112	1 = fighter
-212	2 = dive-bomber
-312	3 = bomber
-412	4 = training
-512	(5 = cancelled)
-612	6 = catapult launch
-712	7 = bomber
-812	8 = reconnaissance
-912	9 = transport

Figure 3

Section A shows generic self-explanatory stencils applied to IJN airframes which varied in size according to aircraft type and manufacturer.

Section B shows the intended type-marker for the first digit for aircraft with a three-numeral tail number. This system was decreed by Aviation Headquarters within the Ministry of Navy (*Koku Honbu*) but in practical terms was often over-ruled in the field. Nonetheless certain consistencies held true: i.e. all Vals were numbered in the 200s series, Bettys in the 300s series and transports in the 900s series.

Figure 4 - MARKINGS

C COWL STENCILS

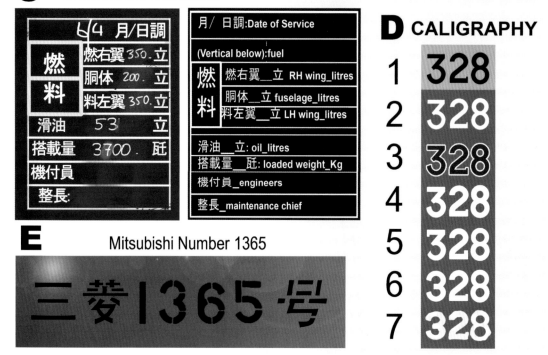

E Mitsubishi Number 1365

Figure 4

Section C decodes the cowl stencil sometimes applied to the port side of the Val's cowl, with the corresponding translation schematic alongside. This marking more commonly appeared on carrier based D3A2 Vals into which was chalked oil and fuel loadings, signed off by the maintenance chief.

Section D shows some of the more common calligraphy styles which appeared in the theatre: 1. black numerals on light background; 2. standard white on camouflage; 3. red with or without white piping; 4. thick white with standard serifs; 5. thick white with accentuated serifs; 6. thick white with different style numeral "3"; 7. thick hand-painted with serifs.

Section E shows the Mitsubishi manufacturer's stencil as applied to sections of the internal airframe, in this case a Model 11 Betty. The glossy blue *aotake* (青竹) colour was universally applied by Mitsubishi to their internal airframes as a corrosion-resistant coating. Similar stencils were applied to most other IJN aircraft types by their manufacturers, often on the fin or rudder.

Figure 5

IJN LAND-BASED & FLYING BOAT UNITS
(Exlcuding floatplane & Zero units)
SOUTH SEAS 1942-1944

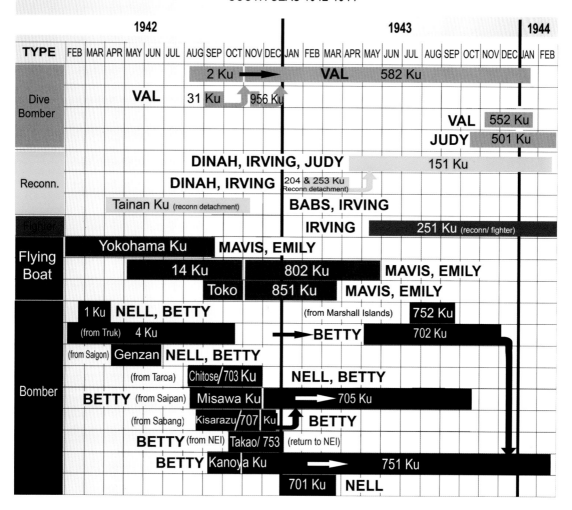

Figure 5

This chronological table shows the deployment timeframes of all IJN land-based and flying boat units deployed to the South Seas theatre. This excludes Zero fighter and floatplane units (covered separately in *Volumes Five* and *Eight* of *Pacific Profiles*).

The tail markings of No. 1 Ku Mitsubishi G6M1-L tail code Z-985, as depicted in Profile 3.

CHAPTER 2
No. 1/752 *Kokutai*

The No. 1 *Kokutai* was activated on 10 April 1941, and became No. 752 *Ku* in the IJN restructure of 1 November 1942. It was based in Taiwan just prior to the Philippines invasion, then moved briefly to Davao before it was called forward to Rabaul via Truk in late February 1942. It operated at Rabaul for just over a month through to 10 April 1942.

The unit was sent to Rabaul following the loss of nearly two *chutai* of No. 4 *Ku* Bettys stemming from the catastrophic attack against the USS *Lexington* on 20 February 1942. Since the bomber unit nearest to Rabaul was No. 1 *Ku*, located in the Marshall Islands, two *chutai* of its Nells were called forward to Vunakanau to temporarily replace the losses. The initial deployment comprised eleven of the unit's 28 Nells. These Nells departed the Marshalls for the first stage of the journey on the morning of 21 February, and their first mission from Vunakanau unfolded on 24 February, a morning reconnaissance of Buna.

Five days later the detachment flew its first bombing mission in the South Seas when seven Nells attacked Port Moresby, the first of several raids against that target during March 1942. Other New Guinea locations attacked during this period included Lae, Bulolo and Madang.

By April No. 1 *Ku* was now operating at full strength with an inventory of 27 Nells, however, with No. 4 *Ku* back to strength, No. 1 *Ku* was reassigned to the 24th Air Flotilla at Taroa in the Central Pacific, its job done. The last Nell departed Rabaul on 10 April 1942, and No. 1 *Ku* left the South Seas theatre for good, at least under this title.

The unit became No. 752 *Ku* in the IJN restructure on 1 November 1942 while still based in the Marshall Islands, during which the unit's fighter wing was formed into a separate fighter *kokutai*, No. 201 *Ku* (see *Pacific Profiles Volume Five*). The unit had meanwhile converted to Bettys in mid-1942, two *buntai* of which it deployed for two months to Rabaul from July to September 1943.

Following the US Marine landings in the middle Solomons from July 1943, a detachment of No. 752 *Ku* Bettys was called forward to Rabaul from the Marshall Islands on 11 July 1943, largely due to its specialist night fighting abilities. Nos. 1 and 2 *Buntai* each sent eleven Bettys to Vunakanau (nine plus two spares), as follows:

> No.1 *Buntai* – tail nos. W2-301, 302, 303, 305, 307, 308, 311, 312, 315, 316 and 317.

> No.2 *Buntai* – tail nos. W-321, 322, 323, 325, 332, 333, 325, 326, 327, 328 and 332

For its first month at Rabaul the detachment mainly conducted daylight attacks against targets in the central Solomons during which it suffered its only crew loss, being FCPO Fujimoto Yoshiharo whose crew went missing over Guadalcanal on 17 July 1943. Then, in August 1943 select crews led by No. 2 *Buntai chutaicho* Lieutenant Nonaka Goro made a series of anti-shipping night strikes, the most eventful of which unfolded on evening of 15 August. Late that afternoon Nonaka led seven No. 2 *Buntai* Bettys from Vunakanau flying tail code W2-321 himself. They refueled at Buin before heading to Barakoma only forty minutes away. Nonaka's Bettys kept up intermittent attacks against US shipping and all returned to Buin by 2325. FCPO Yamamoto Sei'ichi, with two injured crew, force-landed at Buin at 2130 where the bomber was destroyed. The detachment returned to the Marshalls in September 1943.

Markings

During China theatre aerial operations, the IJN implemented a practice of applying tail stripes to distinguish the various *buntai/chutai* within land-based bomber units. The stripes varied in number, width and angle. This markings regimen derived from the logical system of funnel stripes applied to IJN capital ships to visually differentiate similar ships within the same *sentai* (a seafaring battle squadron), according to a ship's assigned numeric position.

The rear fuselage band which appeared on Bettys and Nells during the early months of the Pacific War reflected air flotilla assignment. No. 1 *Ku* replaced the Takao *Ku* when it transferred from the 21st to the 23rd Air Flotilla on 10 April 1941, and the single rear stripe denotes the last digit of this affiliation to the 21st Air Flotilla. In a similar vein, both the Mihoro and Genzan *Ku* bore two stripes from their assignment to the 22nd Air Flotilla. When with the 21st Air Flotilla, No. 1 *Ku* applied diagonal stripes to its fins in order to distinguish it from the Nells in the Kanoya *Ku* which applied a system of horizontal stripes to denote *buntai* assignments. By the time the No. 1 *Ku* Nells arrived at Rabaul they were weather worn, with large sections of camouflage worn down to bare metal, as illustrated in the profiles. Note that some bombers had white leading edges painted on the fins. These are not a unit marking, but a visual warning for the dorsal gunner. When operating at Rabaul, the unit's bombers were divided into four administrative *buntai* (termed a *chutai* when flying as an operational formation).

Following the change of the tail code prefix to "W2" from "Z" by mid-1943 the unit's Bettys were allocated identical *buntai* numbers as had been applied to their Nells, and the tail markings system also referenced the *buntai*. Note that there is a sequencing gap between Nos. 2 and 3 *Buntai*:

No.1 *Buntai* W2-301 to 320; one diagonal stripe

No.2 *Buntai* W2-321 to 335; two diagonal stripes

No.3 *Buntai* W2-351 to 365; three diagonal stripes

No.4 *Buntai* W2-366 to 380; one wide and one narrow diagonal stripe

A poor-quality photo of Nell Z-323, although the two tail stripes of No. 2 Buntai are clearly visible.

The one wide and one narrow diagonal tail stripe indicates Betty W2-373 was assigned to No.4 Buntai of No. 752 Ku.

No. 1/752 KOKUTAI
第一/752 航空隊

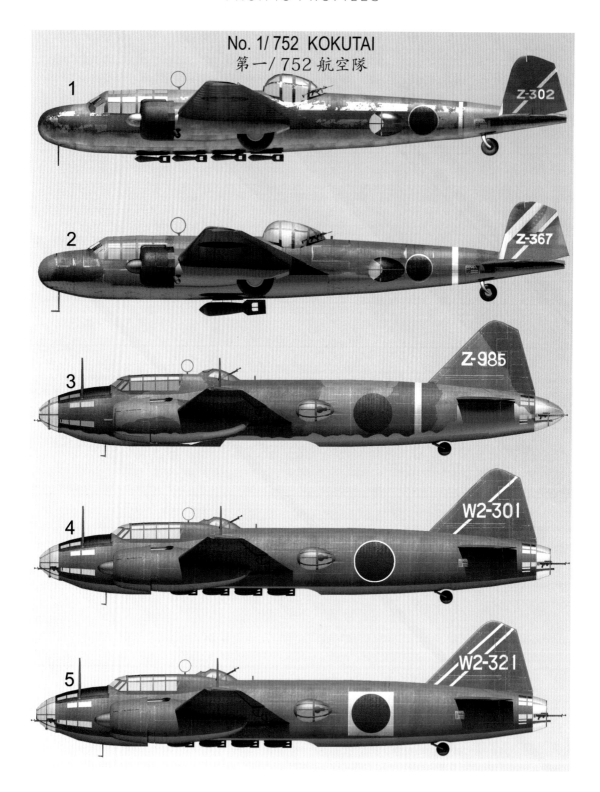

1

Z-302

2

Z-367

3

Z-985

4

W2-301

5

W2-321

Profile 1 – Mitsubishi G3M2 tail code Z-302, No.1 *Buntai*

This bomber is illustrated as it appeared at Rabaul in March 1942. The single stripe indicates assignment to No.1 *Buntai*.

Profile 2 – Mitsubishi G3M2 tail code Z-367, No.4 *Buntai*

This bomber was the only No. 1 *Ku* Nell lost in the South Seas, however its loss was not from combat. The loss occurred during the mid-afternoon of 31 March 1942 when the Nell was approaching Port Moresby in fine weather at 10,000 feet by itself. It exploded over Waigani Swamp, plummeting to the ground in large pieces. Seven bodies were retrieved along with one ceremonial sword. The day previously this same aircraft, identified by the large numerals "67" painted to the underside wing, had ranged over Port Moresby at low altitude by itself. The crew, commanded by FPO1c Harada Takeo, had previously force-landed in the Philippines on 12 December 1941 after being hit by anti-aircraft fire. The crew was captured, and when they were listed as missing in action all were posthumously promoted one rank according to IJN practice. However, when the Japanese invaded the Philippines, the crew was released from custody. When returned to their unit, they were segregated for morale purposes, and continually allocated the most vulnerable battle positions. Despite the odds the crew kept returning, and their survival became sufficiently embarrassing such that Admiral Onishi Takijiro, Chief of Staff of the Naval Aeronautics Bureau, ordered them to attack Port Moresby and not come back. It appears that the bomber's demise was due to detonation of a solitary 250-kilogram bomb, as illustrated here.

Profile 3 – Mitsubishi G6M1-L tail code Z-985, Transport *Buntai*

This early Betty left the Mitsubishi factory in the two-tone "China Scheme", designated as a G6M1-L experimental gunship. The gunship concept was not implemented, however, and the gap in the lower fuselage is the space from where a defensive gondola was removed. The aircraft was then converted into a transport/paratroop carrier, and the 900-series tail number denotes the transport role. No. 1 *Ku* operated this aircraft only briefly before it was reassigned to the Tainan *Ku* also for use in the transport role (see Profile 66). Note the over-painted original tail suffix 181 from its experimental days as a gunship, and the serifs on the prefix "Z". No. 1 *Ku* operated two of these converted transports, the other being tail code Z-986, both of which assisted the move of personnel and logistics for the Rabaul deployment.

Profile 4 – Mitsubishi G4M1 Model 11 W2-301, No. 1 *Buntai*, Lieutenant Natsume Heihachirou

Chutaicho Lieutenant Natsume Heihachirou flew this No. 752 *Ku* Betty when he led strikes against the Rendova area in July/August 1943.

Profile 5 – Mitsubishi G4M1 Model 11 W2-321 No. 2 *Buntai* Lieutenant Nonaka Goro

Chutaicho Lieutenant Nonaka Goro flew this No. 752 *Ku* Betty when he led the night shipping attack mission over the Rendova area on 15 August 1943.

A still image from film of No. 582 Ku's T3-257 departing Buin in April 1943, as illustrated in Profile 12.

The colour scheme on this captured Model 22 Val exemplifies the model's dark green factory camouflage scheme.

CHAPTER 3
No. 2/582 *Kokutai*

Formed in Yokosuka as a mixed dive-bomber and fighter unit headed by *hikocho* Commander Yamamoto Sakae, fifteen Model 32 Zeros assigned to No. 2 *Ku*'s fighter wing arrived at Rabaul on 6 August 1942. These were alongside around nineteen D3A1 Vals, reassigned from No. 33 *Ku* in the Philippines. The *chutaicho* of No. 2 *Ku*'s dive-bomber detachment was Lieutenant Inoue Buntou.

Despite their short range, nine No. 2 *Ku* Vals were deployed against Guadalcanal the following day of 7 August on a one-way mission due to limited range, toting ineffectual 60-kilogram bombs. All nine airframes were lost to either combat or ditchings. The unit then fought hard during the Milne Bay campaign and at one stage based a limited Val detachment at Buna airfield. In October 1942 it commenced missions from both Buin and Buka. These were co-ordinated closely with the Vals of No. 31 *Ku*, often as joint missions. As mounting losses combined with serviceability issues, throughout this phase the detachment struggled to get a full *chutai* airborne, with the maximum number of Vals aloft being eight.

When No. 2 *Ku* was renamed No. 582 *Ku* on 1 November 1942, the unit's cadre continued to refer to itself as the "Yamamoto *Butai*", reflecting the leadership of *hikocho* Commander Yamamoto Sakae. From mid-1943 it called itself the "Inoue *Butai*" when No. 582 *Ku*'s Zero component was disbanded, and it became solely a dive-bomber unit.

During the final weeks of 1942 No. 582 *Ku* Vals were operating from various bases throughout New Guinea and the Solomons. Another dive-bomber unit, No. 956 *Ku* (No. 40 *Ku* prior to the IJN restructure), arrived at Rabaul on 10 November 1942 with ten Vals. The unit was a detachment from the full parent *kokutai* which continued to operate under the 2nd Southern Expeditionary Fleet in Singapore and the Netherlands East Indies. After flying missions in the Buna area, the detachment was absorbed by No. 582 *Ku* where it continued to operate as its own *buntai*.

The loss rate of airframes accelerated exponentially in the first quarter of 1943 with *chutaicho* Lieutenant Kitamura Norimasa lost when leading a fifteen Val mission on 1 February against shipping off Tulagi. He was replaced by Lieutenant Miyazaki Yu'ichiro who was himself killed a short time later on 28 March 1943 when leading another substantive mission of eighteen Vals. Miyazaki in turn was replaced by Lieutenant Takahata Tatsuo with the Solomons detachment still based at Buin.

Among the replacement Vals delivered to Rabaul in late October 1942 was a batch of the first Model 22s, which had begun leaving the Japanese factory in August 1942. These were able to carry one 250-kilogram bomb slung under the fuselage and two wing-mounted 60-kilogram bombs, a common ordnance loading from Buin as operations ventured into 1943. No. 582 *Ku*'s last mission from Rabaul took place on 14 January 1944 after which the handful of surviving Vals were evacuated to Truk.

Markings

Combined Fleet orders assigned both No. 2 *Ku*'s fighter and dive-bomber contingents the tail prefix "Q". Since the initial batch of Vals delivered to Rabaul had previously served with No. 33 *Ku* in the Philippines, the "33" prefix codes were painted over and replaced with codes Q-201 to Q-219, hand-painted in white. Replacement aircraft later ferried to Rabaul were allocated incremental tail codes; evidence suggests tail codes of aircraft lost were not replicated. Since the detachment initially operated as one *chutai*, there was no need for separate *chutai* colours. Following the loss of nine airframes on 7 August 1942, the unit lost four more to combat by the end of September, with an unknown number of non-combat losses, reducing the remaining half dozen or so to anti-submarine patrols or solo reconnaissance missions.

When restructured as No. 582 *Ku* on 1 November 1942, the unit maintained separate fighter and dive-bomber contingents, although No. 582 *Ku*'s fighter wing was detached from its parent 22nd Air Flotilla. For the rest of its time in the South Seas until mid-1943, No. 582 *Ku* Zeros were rotated between Rabaul's air flotillas on a roving commission (both Nos. 252 and 582 *Ku* comprised the First Air Attack Force, and in doing so they adopted a unique tail code system as outlined in *Pacific Profiles Volume Five*). During 1942, No. 2 *Ku*'s Zeros had adopted a single red or blue chevron as its unit marking according to *chutai*, with a double chevron indicating *chutaicho* status. This chevron marking was unique in the theatre and continued with No. 582 *Ku*.

Meanwhile, No. 582 *Ku*'s dive-bombers remained attached to the 26th Air Flotilla and were assigned the associated tail prefix "T3", replacing the previous "Q" prefix codes and in some cases accompanied by chevrons as used by the Zeros. By February 1943 at Buin the tail codes lay in the T3-224 and T3-266 range, painted in red. The Model 22 Vals and later batches of Model 11s left the factory in overall green. Earlier grey Model 11s were painted overall green in the field, making the red chevron as applied in New Guinea difficult to see in black and white photos.

At the beginning of 1943 the Vals operated in different detachments with the No. 1 *Chutai* (the Inoue *chutai* - red) based either at Rabaul or New Guinea, and the No. 2 *Chutai* (the Kitamura *chutai*, later the Miyazaki and Takahata *chutai* - yellow) at Buin. Around May 1943, in a decision to increase visibility the tail codes were repainted in either white or yellow.

The "T3" prefix was replaced by the single prefix "2" in mid-1943 for reasons which remain unclear as No. 582 *Ku*'s Val wing retained the same flotilla association. In August 1943, No. 582 *Ku* became purely a dive-bomber unit, with its Zero fighters transferred to No. 204 *Ku*. In addition, No. 582 *Ku* also absorbed several Model 22s and crews from the 2nd Air Flotilla (*Junyo*, *Hiyo* and *Ryuho*) when these carrier air wings, now land-based and operating from Buin and Rabaul, withdrew from the South Seas to reorganise (Profile 8 showcases an example of an early previous carrier airframe).

In December 1943 the prefix was again changed, this time to "82", the reason being the arrival of another Val unit in the theatre, No. 552 *Ku*. This unit also had the numeral two as its last digit, so the two units employed prefixes "82" and "52" to avoid confusion. A curiosity to the four tail code series for No. 582 *Ku* Model 22s is that all appear to have been hand-painted, instead of stencilled.

Val Model 22s taxi at Vunakanau. Note the numeral 4 on the spat.

D3A2 Model 22 tail code 82-224, as depicted in Profile 16, lies abandoned at Cape Hoskins.

No. 2/ 582 KOKUTAI
第二／582 航空隊

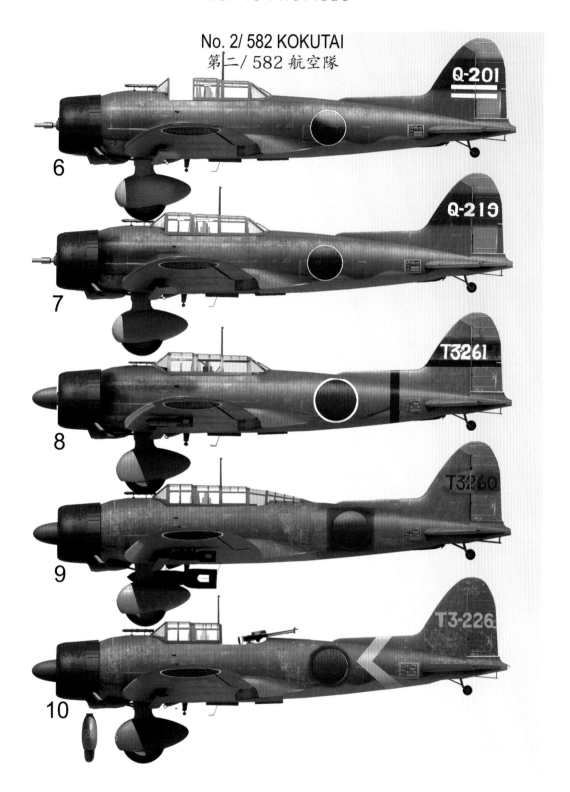

6

7

8

9

10

Profile 6 – Aichi D3A1 tail code Q-201, *Chutaicho* Lieutenant Inoue Buntou

The *chutaicho* of No. 2 *Ku*'s dive-bomber detachment was pilot Lieutenant Inoue Buntou. This profile is theoretical, on the likely assumption that Inoue followed IJN markings practice of the times of securing the first issued tail code as his own and then applying double horizontal markings to indicate his status as *chutaicho*. Note however that no photograph of his Val has surfaced to date.

Profile 7 – Aichi D3A1 MN 3114, tail code Q-219, FPO1c Maruyama Takeshi

After trying to find two Australian ships off Milne Bay in marginal weather on 2 September 1942, three No. 2 *Ku* Vals force-landed on an isolated New Guinea beach after running low on fuel. The six crew were eventually killed by an Australian patrol. Aware of the dangers of turning over when ditching the Val with its fixed gear, the trio elected to land on a beach. The stranded crews subsequently set off to return to Japanese-occupied Buna, after setting fire to their beached aircraft. Nonetheless, Allied intelligence was able to extensively examine the wreckage of all three aircraft. Q-219, flown by FPO1c Maruyama Takeshi, has a hand-painted tail code applied over a previous No. 33 *Ku* code. The profile is created from photos of the three Vals taken by Allied intelligence.

Profile 8 – Aichi D3A1 MN 3470, tail code T3-261, Ensign Nomura Harumi and Lieutenant (jg) Okamura Teinosuke

This No. 582 *Ku* profile is created from photos and technical reports of wreckage taken at Munda in August 1943. Note that, as a late model D3A1 manufactured in June 1942, this Val has a spinner. The tail code T3-261 was painted over the previous *Hiyo* tail code in the D1- 2XX format. The single red band and red horizontal *shotaicho* stripe are legacy markings from this previous assignment. The fact that No. 582 *Ku* chose to retain its *shotaicho* stripe indicates this Val was likely a regular mount of either or both Ens Nomura Harumi and/or Lieutenant (jg) Okamura Teinosuke, both of whom were active in the unit's operations from Buin in the first half of 1943.

Profile 9 – D3A2 Model 22 MN 3106, tail code T3-260

This profile is created from photos and technical reports of the wreckage of the airframe taken at Munda in August 1943. The fuselage *hinomaru* was originally surrounded by a white square that has been painted out with dark green, a common practice in the field during this period. This Val left the factory in June 1942, and note that on this particular No. 2 *Chutai* airframe the tail code has exceptionally been applied in red.

Profile 10 – D3A2 Model 22 MN 3125, tail code T3-226

This airframe was examined in December 1943 where it was shot down over the small island of Mbanga (Baanga) near New Georgia in the Solomons. It was assessed to have crashed earlier in July of that year, and the Allied field report documents the yellow chevron painted on the rear fuselage.

No. 582 KOKUTAI
第582 航空隊

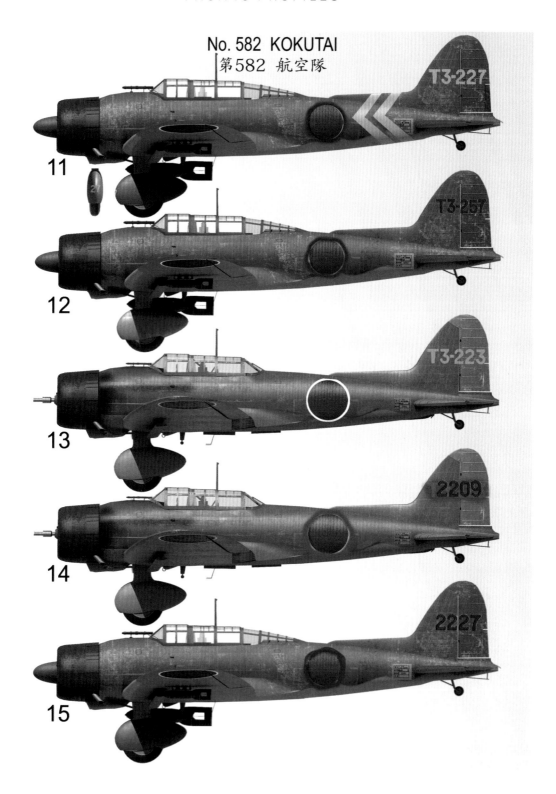

Profile 11 – D3A2 Model 22 tail code T3-227, Lieutenant (jg) Okamura Teinosuke

This Model 22 was used as the lead aircraft for missions from Buin throughout February/ March 1943, and was regularly crewed with senior observers such as Lieutenant (jg) Okamura Teinosuke or other officer ranks. As such it was marked with a double chevron to denote its *chutaicho* role. Okamura led an afternoon anti-shipping mission on 10 February 1943 from this dive-bomber which resulted another participant T3-237 making an emergency landing at Munda where it was repaired before returning to Buin the following day. On this same mission T3-241 made an emergency landing back at Buin after aborting the mission and dumping its 250-kilogram bomb into the ocean.

Profile 12 – D3A2 Model 22 tail code T3-257

This Model 22 was filmed departing Buin in April 1943. The *hinomaru* white surround has been painted over.

Profiles 13 & 14 – D3A1 Model 11 MN 3237, tail codes T3-223 & 2209

Manufactured in August 1941, Profile 13 illustrates the aircraft just after it was assigned into the unit before the white surround on the *hinomaru* was painted over. This Model 11 was renumbered 2209 in mid-1943 when the unit changed its tail prefix (as per Profile 14) and was ultimately abandoned at Lae following battle damage where it was analysed by Allied intelligence in September 1943.

Profile 15 – D3A2 Model 22 MN 3023 tail code 2227

This Model 22 was manufactured in October 1942 and was abandoned at Lae following battle damage. It was inspected by Allied intelligence in September 1943.

The tail of Aichi D3A1 tail code T3-261, as illustrated in Profile 8, at Munda.

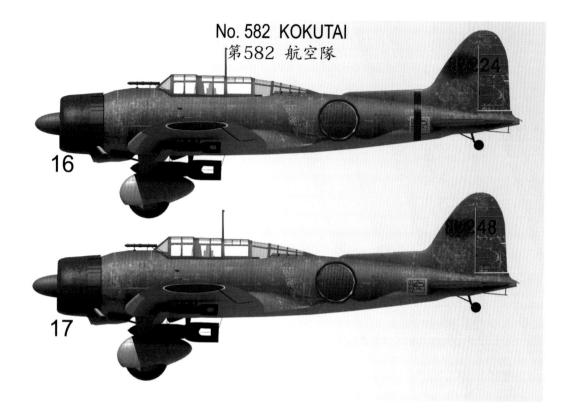

No. 582 KOKUTAI
第582 航空隊

16

17

Profile 16 – D3A2 Model 22 tail code 82-224

This Model 22 was transferred from the *Hiyo* air wing around mid-1943. It was abandoned after it force-landed at Cape Hoskins on New Britain in late 1943, following battle damage incurred during one of the December 1943 shipping strikes at Cape Merkus. The airframe was surveyed by US intelligence in September 1944. The red fuselage band is a legacy marking from its *Hiyo* days.

Profile 17 – D3A2 Model 22 MN 3357, tail code 82-248

This airframe was abandoned at Gasmata in December 1943 following another of the late 1943 Cape Merkus missions.

The wreckage of T3-260, as shown in Profile 9, at Munda. Just visible is the painted-out white square around the hinomaru.

The unusually shaped tail code of Val Q-219, the subject of Profile 7, as examined by Allied intelligence.

The tail of Q-218 as over-painted on the previous No. 33 Ku tail code.

Its buntai affiliation indicated by the three stripes on its tail, this Chitose Ku No. 3 Buntai Nell is seen in the Marshall Islands in late 1941.

A formation of Chitose Ku Nells on approach to Rabaul on 16 January 1942.

CHAPTER 4
Chitose/No. 703 *Kokutai*

The Chitose *Ku* was known within the IJN as the "Ohashi Butai" after its commanding officer, Captain Ohashi Fujiro. It was established at Chitose, Hokkaido, on 1 October 1939 with an inventory of G3M2 Nells. Commencing in June 1941, and assigned to the 24th Air Flotilla, the *kokutai* trained in the Japanese Pacific mandates including Saipan, Palau and the Marshall Islands. In late November 1941 it advanced to Kwajalein Atoll with a strength of four *buntai* comprising three dozen bombers and a separate fighter wing of eighteen A5M Claude fighters. From these inventories, detachments were then dispersed to Truk and Tarawa.

Shortly before the commencement of the Pacific War, the Chitose *Ku* bomber wing was assigned two new G4M1s which supplemented three dozen Nells. The Bettys were used judiciously to conduct fleet escort and undertake reconnaissance missions from October 1941. After the Pacific War was declared, the *kokutai* attacked Wake Island during December 1941.

Early in January 1942, eighteen Nells from Nos. 1 and 4 *Buntai* were dispatched to Truk specifically to conduct operations against Rabaul in preparation for its invasion, whilst Nos. 2 and 3 *Buntai* remained in the Marshall Islands. The exception was the two Bettys, their long range used for reconnaissance purposes from Truk. In the event, Chitose *Ku* Nells conducted only three bombing missions against Rabaul on 4, 7 and 16 January.

After fully converting to the Betty around mid-1942, the Chitose *Ku* sent two *chutai* of Bettys to Rabaul in late August 1942. This detachment flew its first bombing strike from Vunakanau against Guadalcanal on 4 September. Whilst at Rabaul, the Chitose *Ku* was rebadged as No. 703 *Ku* on 1 November 1942. As the Chitose *Ku*, it had already lost three Bettys over Guadalcanal before the administrative transition, however it proceeded to lose most of its remaining airframes under the No. 703 *Ku* umbrella, a further ten Bettys. The most disastrous loss occurred on 12 November when eight out of a *chutai* of nine attacking Guadalcanal were shot down by Wildcats. A patrol on 14 November comprised the final South Seas mission by No. 703 *Ku*. The handful of survivors was recalled to Truk the following day.

Markings

The unit was allocated the tail code "S" within the 24th Air Flotilla. During the 1941 era in the Pacific mandates the unit operated several Nells in NMF without camouflage. Several were *hokoku* aircraft including HK-398 (第一鴻池號 – the first airframe donated by the Konoike Corporation). As outlined in Chapter 2, by the time of the Pacific War the IJN implemented a practice of applying tail stripes to distinguish the various *buntai/chutai* within land-based bomber units. The stripes used by the Chitose *Ku* derived from the logical system of funnel stripes which delineated IJN capital ships. The Chitose *Ku* applied a system of horizontal stripes to indicate *buntai* assignment to its Nells and Bettys thus:

No. 1 *Buntai*, one thin stripe, tail codes S-301 to S-320

No. 2 *Buntai*, two thin stripes, tail codes S-321 to S-340

No. 3 *Buntai*, three stripes, tail codes S-341 to S-360

No. 4 *Buntai*, one thin stripe and one broad one above, tail codes S-361 to S-380

When redesignated as No. 703 *Ku*, the unit prefix was changed from "S" to "W1", a prefix shared with its fighter wing serving in the Marshalls. The *kokutai* was disbanded on 15 March 1943 after which the tail prefix "W1" was reassigned to the Zero fighter unit No. 201 *Ku*.

The civilian version of the Nell promoted by the Mainichi newspaper conducted a world tour in 1939, the same year that the Chitose Ku was established. It is seen here at Tehran airport, Iran.

The tail of G4M1 S-359, as illustrated in Profile 20, as abandoned in the Marshalls.

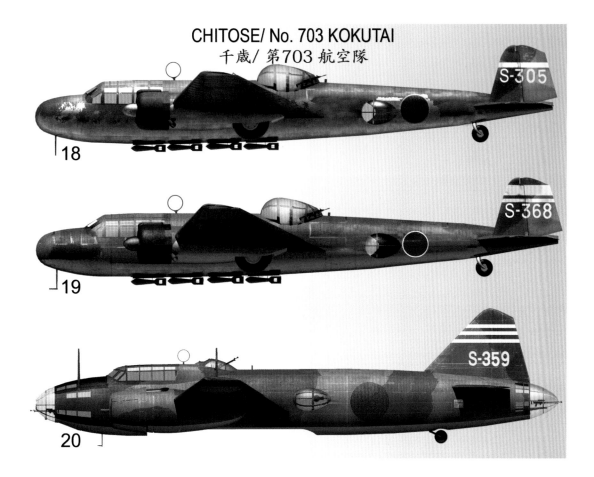

CHITOSE/ No. 703 KOKUTAI
千歳/ 第703 航空隊

S-305

18

S-368

19

S-359

20

Profile 18 – Mitsubishi G3M2 tail code S-305, No.1 *Buntai*

One of the nine Nells from the Chitose *Ku* No. 1 *Buntai* operating from Truk in January 1942 specifically to conduct operations against Rabaul.

Profile 19 – Mitsubishi G3M2 tail code S-368, No.4 *Buntai*

One of the nine Nells from the Chitose *Ku* No. 4 *Buntai* operating from Truk in January 1942 specifically to conduct operations against Rabaul.

Profile 20 – Mitsubishi G4M1 tail code S-359, No.3 *Buntai*, observer Warrant Officer Makino Koushichi

Operated by No. 3 *Buntai*, this G4M1 was used to reconnoitre Rabaul from Truk in December 1941, and also as an advance observer aircraft for the two Rabaul bombing missions on 4 and 16 January 1942. Warrant Officer Makino Koushichi, the seventh child in his family, was a regular aircraft commander for these flights. Note the symmetrical numeral "3" in the tail number. This Betty was later abandoned in the Marshalls.

No. 4 Ku's G4M1 F-322, the subject of Profile 23, on its way to Port Moresby in formation with F-323 and F-325.

Ground crew at Vunakanau wave goodbye to Betty F-352, as depicted in Profile 21, for the landmark first raid against Port Moresby of 28 February 1942.

CHAPTER 5
No. 4 *Kokutai*

This hard-fighting unit suffered the most grievous losses of all IJN bomber units in the South Seas. It was much defined by its commander, Captain Moritama Yoshiyotsu, a non-aviator charged with building the group to full strength and bringing it to Rabaul. Moritama had been a communications officer aboard the battleship *Haruna* in late 1939 before he was transferred to the training unit Yatabe *Ku* as commander in March 1941. He was then transferred to No. 4 *Ku*, and later oversaw the transition to No. 702 *Ku* after the unit was returned to Japan during the November 1942 IJN restructure. This unit is treated separately in Chapter 22 due to its seven-month reformation and absence from the theatre whilst in Japan.

No. 4 *Ku* was created as a joint bomber/fighter unit. The genesis of its origins stems back to 27 November 1941 when fifteen fighter pilots arrived at Truk where they would serve as No. 4 *Ku*'s fighter wing, at first serving under the umbrella of the Chitose *Ku*. The *hikotaicho* of the bomber wing was Lieutenant Commander Ito Takuzo. The unit moved to its new base at Rabaul shortly after its capture in January 1942. The combined *kokutai* became known colloquially around Rabaul as the "F *Kokutai*" due to its tail prefix, or the "Moritama Kokutai". It retained this moniker even after it returned to Rabaul in May 1943 as No. 702 *Ku* in the way of IJN tradition.

The *kokutai* was established with headquarters at Rabaul on 10 February 1942, where the bomber wing was initially allocated two complete *chutai* of G4M1 Bettys, comprising 22 bombers which included four held as reserves. Their crews, recently transferred from the Takao *Ku*, were later joined by a third *chutai* commandeered from the Chitose *Ku* detachment in the Marianas.

The *hikotaicho* Ito arrived from Truk on 11 February 1942 leading a trio of former Takao *Ku* bombers: F-348, F-350 and F-354. The very first Betty reconnaissance of Port Moresby had been conducted that same morning by two Bettys which had arrived from Truk the day before. On the fine-weather morning of 28 February, a combined formation of seven G3M2 Nells and eleven G4M1 Bettys, from Nos. 1 and 4 *Ku* respectively headed for Port Moresby.

This third *chutai* (ex-Chitose *Ku*) was rushed to Vunakanau following the severe losses sustained during the attack on the USS *Lexington* of 20 February 1942. Led by Lieutenant Yamagata Shigeo, ten bombers made the journey individually, and after each taking four to five hours flight time, they touched down at Vunakanau mid-afternoon. On 14 March 1942 eight Bettys raided against Horn Island, in what constituted a landmark first bombing attack against Australia from a South Seas base.

As part of the 1 April 1942 restructure, the 25th Air Flotilla was created in Rabaul to assume control of South Seas air operations. In the process No. 4 *Ku* was transformed into a bomber outfit, and its fighter wing was transferred to the Tainan *Ku*. The new unit was increased in strength to four *chutai* of 36 Betty bombers with several spares. To make up the bomber force, nine crews were transferred from No. 1 *Ku* and five more from the Kisarazu *Ku*.

The unit suffered grievous losses during the two opening days of the Guadalcanal campaign, on 7 and 8 August 1942, and was able to operate only piecemeal throughout the rest of August and September. During the eight months it served in the South Seas it lost 55 Bettys to combat and operations. Its personnel losses in the South Seas included two *hikotaicho*, six *buntaicho*, and the equivalent of 42 crews. By 25 September 1942, the survivors had been reduced to six Bettys which returned to Kisarazu via Truk with their crews to regroup.

Markings

The first *chutai* of Bettys to enter the inventory was transferred from the Takao *Ku*'s No. 4 *Buntai* and lay in the F-346 to 359 range, including four confirmed tail codes F-352 (ex T-352), F-348 (ex T-348), F-350 (ex T-350) and F-354 (ex T-354). All wore the brown and green *kumogata* (cloud pattern) camouflage scheme, and No. 4 *Ku* replaced the white "T" tail prefix with an "F" a few days after arriving in Rabaul, retaining the last three digits of the original Takao *Ku* number. Several Takao *Ku* officers were also transferred to No. 4 *Ku*.

When No. 4 *Ku* was restructured into a bomber unit of four *buntai/chutai*, its allocations were:

No. 1 *Buntai*	F-301 to 320 (no fin stripes)
No. 2 *Buntai*	F-321 to 340 (one fin stripe)
No. 3 *Buntai*	F-341 to 360 (two fin stripes)
No. 4 *Buntai*	F-361 to 380 (one thin and one thick fin stripe)

Subsequent to the substantial losses incurred during August 1942, bombers were often transferred between units at short notice without time to reapply revised *buntai* markings, resulting in several tail codes which did not align to the above structure.

F-319 from No. 4 Ku's No. 1 Buntai over the South Seas post May 1942.

The wreck of Betty F-331 at Lae. This is an early all-green bomber with no white background or piping on the hinomaru.

The wreck of Betty F-356 at Lae showcases the two fin stripes representing No.3 Buntai.

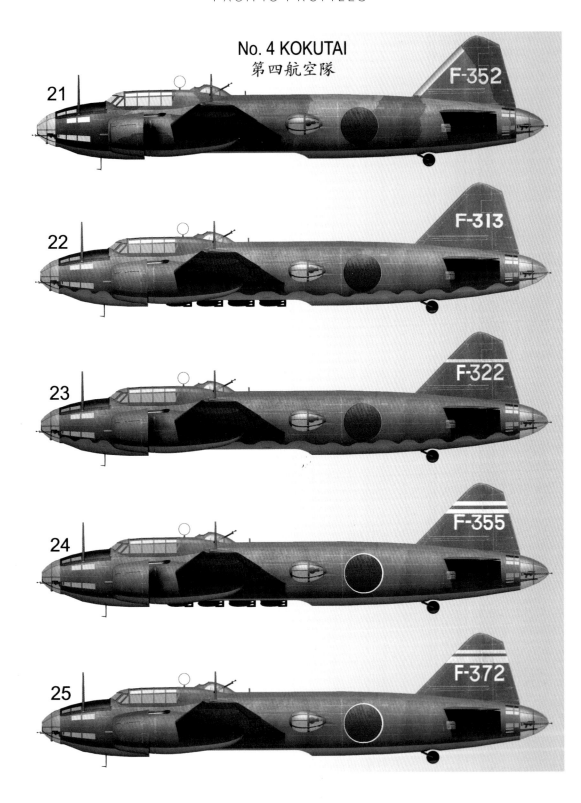

No. 4 KOKUTAI
第四航空隊

F-352

F-313

F-322

F-355

F-372

Profile 21 – Mitsubishi G4M1 tail code F-352 (former T-352)

This Betty is one of the ex-Takao *Ku* allocation which subsequently participated in the first air-raid against Port Moresby on 28 February 1942, as seen in a movie taken of it departing Vunakanau. The leading edge on the fin is a replaced aluminium panel from a field repair, and not a painted unit marking.

Profile 22 – Mitsubishi G4M1 tail code F-313, No. 1 *Buntai*

This all-green Betty carries a wavy camouflage demarcation line which was apparent among the first batches of Bettys which left the Mitsubishi factory in overall green. This replacement aircraft arrived in the inventory around late March 1942.

Profile 23 – Mitsubishi G4M1 tail code F-322, No. 2 *Buntai*

Photographed on its way to Port Moresby in April 1942, this No. 4 *Ku* No. 2 *Buntai* Betty is another which has the wavy camouflage demarcation line from Mitsubishi's first batches of the overall green scheme.

Profile 24 – Mitsubishi G4M1 tail code F-355, No. 3 *Buntai*, pilot FPO1c Daisen Chiharu

This Betty was shot down by Airacobras during a bombing raid against Port Moresby on 18 May 1942, and crashed into mountainous terrain about nineteen miles from Seven-Mile 'drome. The tail number is recorded in the unit's operations log, and wreckage at the sight shows the *hinomaru* had white piping. The straight camouflage demarcation line indicates it is a replacement Betty from around early May 1942.

Profile 25 – Mitsubishi G4M1 tail code F-372, No. 4 *Buntai*

The white piping on the *hinomaru* and straight camouflage demarcation line indicates F-372 is another replacement aircraft from around May 1942 onwards.

The wreck of No. 802 Ku Emily N1-16 as destroyed on the shore of Malaguna, Rabaul, by US air attacks.

Emily N1-13, as depicted in Profile 29, being loaded aboard the seaplane tender Akitsushima in Rabaul harbour in early 1943.

CHAPTER 6
No. 14/802 *Kokutai*

The first generation of No. 14 *Ku* operated in the China theatre. It was headquartered in Taiwan as a shore-based unit but was deactivated on 15 September 1941. Following the April 1942 IJN restructure, the second generation was reactivated as a flying boat unit on 10 April 1942 at Yokosuka and assigned to the 24th Air Flotilla.

Throughout its South Seas service, the No. 14 *Ku* commanding officer was Commander Nakajima Daizo. The unit's H8K2 Emily flying boats were based at Jaluit in the Marshall Islands, however they visited Rabaul frequently commencing in May 1942. Outside the scope of this volume, the unit created a separate fighter wing on 20 September 1942 equipped with Rufes (see *Pacific Profiles Volume Eight*).

In July 1942, a detachment of Mavises was sent to the Shortland Islands to conduct long-range reconnaissance patrols of the Solomons. In addition, a detachment of four Emilys arrived at Rabaul from Jaluit, tail codes W-37, W-45, W-46 and W-47. On the late evening of 25 July 1942, W-45 and W-46 bombed Townsville, Australia, and loitered overhead into the early hours of the next morning. The raid was repeated two days later by W-46, and then on 28 July by W-47 (after the accompanying W-37 returned to base with technical problems). This last raid was the most eventful, with Lieutenant Shoji Kingo forced to evade attacks by USAAF Airacobras.

On 1 November 1942 No. 14 *Ku* was redesignated as No. 802 *Ku* and placed under the direct command of the 11th Air Fleet with the revised tail code prefix "N1". With most of its inventory then based at the Shortland Islands, commanding officer Nakajima continued his duties, until later replaced by Lieutenant Commander Suzuki Yoshijiro from 1 March 1943. Suzuki was in turn replaced by Rear Admiral Kamo Yuhao on 1 December 1943 who served until 13 February 1944.

Following a lull in USN air attacks against southern Bougainville, on 13 March 1943 the unit's fighter wing redeployed to Jaluit. A Mavis escorted the thirteen remaining airworthy Rufes to their new distant destination via Kavieng, Truk and Ponape, a journey lasting several days. The smaller inventory of Mavis and Emilys also subsequently moved operations there, however they continued to visit Rabaul and the Shortlands as late as May 1943. When reassigned to the 22nd Air Flotilla in mid-1943 the unit was assigned the new tail prefix "Y4". However, by then the inventory was stationed at Jaluit. No 802 *Ku* was subsequently decommissioned on 1 April 1944.

No. 14 / 802 KOKUTAI
第十四航空隊

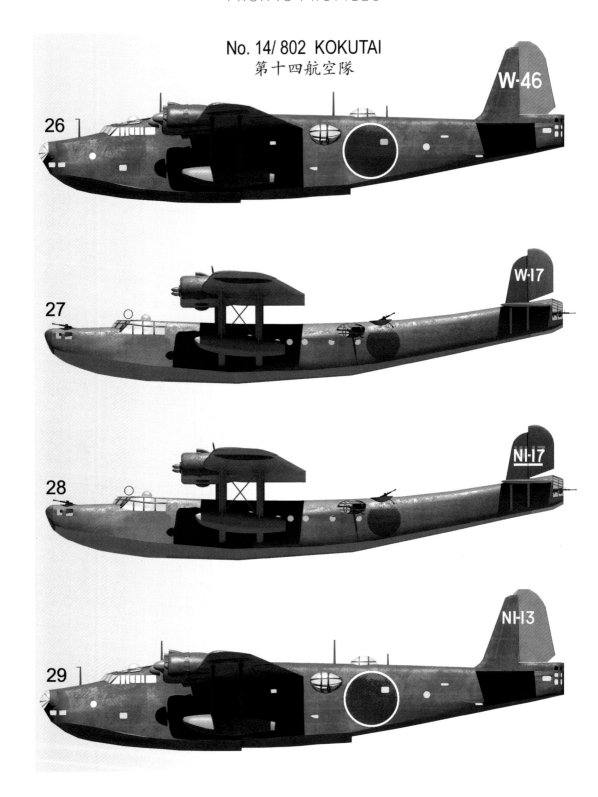

26

W-46

27

W-17

28

NI-17

29

NI-13

Profile 26 – H8K2 Emily tail code W-46, Lieutenant Mizukura Kiyoshi

Mizukura piloted this No. 14 *Ku* Emily over Townsville on the night of 27/28 July 1942.

Profile 27 – H6K4 Mavis tail code W-17

This No. 14 *Ku* Mavis is illustrated as it appeared in the Shortland Islands in July 1942.

Profile 28 – H6K4 Mavis tail code N1-17

This Mavis is the same aircraft as W-17 (see Profile 27, above) illustrated as it later appeared at Rabaul around December 1942. The revised No. 802 *Ku* "N1" prefix issued by the 11th Air Fleet has been applied over the previous tail code W-17, with a *chutaicho* stripe added under the code.

Profile 29 – H8K2 Emily tail code N1-13

This No. 802 *Ku* Emily is illustrated as it appeared being loaded aboard the seaplane tender *Akitsushima* in Rabaul's Simpson Harbour in early 1943.

The tail of Emily Y4-2X as applied over the previous 11th Air Fleet "N1" prefix. The last digit is unknown; however, it cannot be N1-29 which was shot down in 1943. The prefix "Y4" was applied after No. 802 Ku had departed from the South Seas.

not applied or painted over for security purposes. The unit commenced numbering its airframes in the 50 series. Photos of the unit's two Judys disclose tail numbers 51 and 52, and one of the Irving shows T4-57, meaning the four Dinahs were allocated numbers 53 to 56. It is possible they initially displayed the T4 prefix, however photographic evidence on this unit is scant. Whilst the JAAF in the South Seas left its Ki-46s in the Mitsubishi light olive brown, the IJN painted the top half overall green to match its other airframes. This was applied in the field from local paint stocks.

A No. 151 Ku Judy prepares to depart Lakunai, warming its engine near the foothills of the airfield's northern area, with long-range tanks slung under the wings. Ground personnel follow the two embarking aircrew, carrying the observer's charts and navigation gear.

Profile 33 – Ki-46 tail code 54, *hikotaicho* Lieutenant Tokieda Shigeru

One of four Ki-46s supervised by *hikotaicho* Lieutenant Tokieda Shigeru, these reconnaissance Ki-46s often deployed to Buin in southern Bougainville.

Profile 34 – Ki-46 tail code W4-56

This illustration is hypothetical on the possibility that some Ki-46s initially had applied the tail code prefix "W4" as allocated by the 21st Air Flotilla.

Profile 35 – D4Y1 Judy MN 330, tail code 51, pilot FPO2c Maeda Kouyu

This Judy is recorded as missing in IJN records on 15 August 1943, when flown by FPO2c Maeda Kouyu. In fact, it had been shot down by an Allied fighter before crashing into the ocean off Choiseul in the Solomons.

Profile 36 – D4Y1 Judy MN 340, tail code 52, Ensign Koko Yoshio

This Judy was shot down during the late afternoon of 30 August 1943 by a Corsair conducting a high altitude test flight over Guadalcanal.

Profile 37 – Nakajima J1N1 tail code W4-57, Lieutenant (jg) Ashikawa Hideo

Lieutenant (jg) Ashikawa Hideo supervised operation of No. 151 *Ku*'s only Irving, and often flew in the aircraft as observer. It is unclear whether the prefix "W4" was painted out.

No. 151 KOKUTAI
第151航空隊

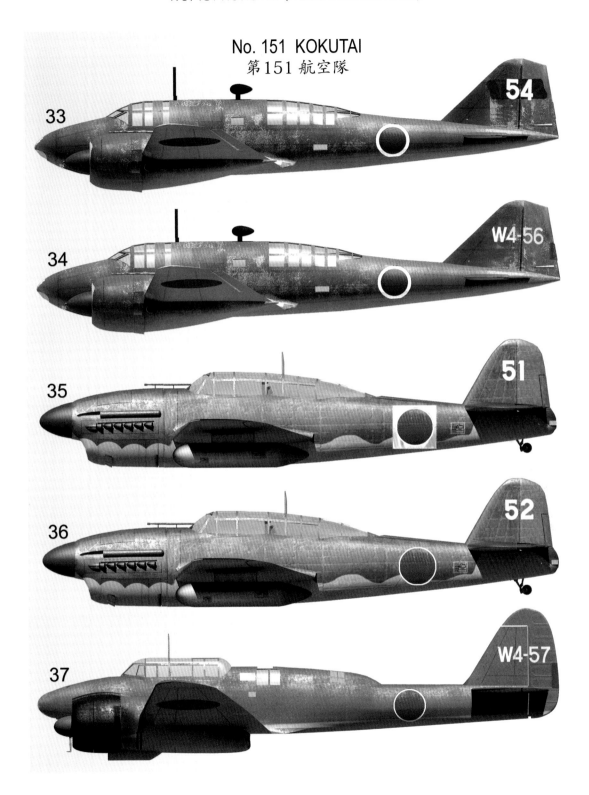

33

54

34

W4-56

35

51

36

52

37

W4-57

Two No. 251 Ku's J1N1-s Irvings head off from Rabaul for night operations against a backdrop of the Mother and Daughter volcanoes.

Field-modified J1N1-c tail code U1-20, as depicted in Profile 39, taxiing at Vunakanau during trials by FCPO Kudo Shigetoshi. The foreground Kasei 15 engine cowl has a canvas exhaust cover with the kanji characters 三二五, indicating this is Betty 325 serving with No. 702 Ku.

CHAPTER 10
No. 251 *Kokutai*

The Tainan *Ku*, operating Zero fighters, had been a South Seas stalwart unit throughout 1942. When it was redesignated as No. 251 *Ku* on 1 November 1942, its handful of survivors returned to Japan the following week to regroup. It retained Captain Kozono Yasuna as *hikocho*, thus maintaining its colloquial name the "Kozono *Butai*". No. 251 *Ku* re-equipped with Model 22 Zeros and its continuing association with the 25th Air Flotilla saw it allocated the new unit prefix "U1".

After some months in Japan, No. 251 *Ku* sailed to Truk from Yokosuka on 25 April 1943 with 58 Zeros aboard the carriers *Unyo* and *Chuyo*. Importantly, the Zero inventory was complemented by two J1N1-c Irving (the "c" indicating reconnaissance) reconnaissance twins and supported logistically by two Nell transports with tail codes U1-901 and U1-902.

Despite its reformation as a Zero fighter unit, the *kokutai* soon became the only South Seas fighter unit to operate the J1N1-s Irving night fighter. The two Irvings accompanying the Zeros back to Rabaul were identical to the first three J1N1-c models operated by the Tainan *Ku*. However, in accordance with Kozono's orders, a third J1N1-c delivered shortly thereafter was field-fitted with ventral and dorsal 20mm cannons. This airframe was then trialed as a night fighter by FCPO Kudo Shigetoshi and Warrant Officer Ono Satoru. Kudo became instrumental in subsequently pushing the Aeronautics Section in the Department of Navy to accept and progress the concept of the Irving as a night fighter.

The unit's first Irving mission was a two-hour reconnaissance from Lakunai on 13 May 1943, and on 18 May the second J1N1-c temporarily took up station at Lae. Throughout May and June 1943, the modified J1N1-c was joined by J1N1-s variants which downed numerous 43rd BG B-17s during night operations over Rabaul. Then, in July 1943 the Irvings ventured further afield to Buin, Buka and Ballale.

Meanwhile, such was the attrition rate of Zeros and experienced pilots that operational leadership defaulted to a junior officer, Lieutenant (jg) Oshibuchi Takashi. The unit continued Zero operations in the Solomons area until 1 September 1943 after which it was reclassified as a twin-engine night fighter unit. The remaining Zero inventory was dispersed among Rabaul's other Zero units, mainly No. 253 *Ku*.

Only modest numbers of night fighter Irvings were deployed to Rabaul, with no more than five being operational at any time. On 19 July 1943 a Ballale based J1N1-s ditched in the early hours following return fire from a B-17, with both crewmen rescued. On 21 October 1943 aircraft commander FPO2c Hareyama Fumio and his pilot went missing in action. Then, in October 1943 Irving MNs 644 and 646 were destroyed on the ground at Rabaul as a result of Allied bombing raids.

In late November 1943 the unit moved operations from Lakunai to Vunakanau due to the pressures of ongoing raids, and by the end of the month No. 251 *Ku* was down to four Irvings at Rabaul and another based at Kavieng. On 2 January 1944 it lost another Irving to an accident, three months prior to the last Irving mission from Rabaul which was flown on 28 March 1944.

Markings

Initially No. 251 *Ku* applied the tail prefix "U1" to its Irvings, including the initial three J1N1-c models, which included confirmed tail codes U1-13 and U1-20. These numbers were applied in Japan and were thus out of sequence. Following the receipt of the J1N1-s airframes, and when the *kokutai* was converted solely to a night fighter unit, the prefix was abolished for security reasons and the tail codes were renumbered, in the hundreds series to denote a fighter unit, commencing at 101. The J1N1-c arrived in theatre in overall green with grey undersurfaces with white piping on the *hinomaru*, whereas the J1N1-s was painted in an overall dark matt green which verged on black.

Profile 38 – Nakajima J1N1-c tail code U1-13

This J1N1-c temporarily took up station at Lae on 18 May 1943. Note the hand-painted "13" on the nose.

Profile 39 – Nakajima J1N1-c tail code U1-20

This J1N1-c was photographed at Lakunai in mid-1943. Note the hand-painted "20" just behind the Perspex nose fitted as part of a hybrid airframe. This was the third J1N1-c assigned to the unit, later field modified at Lakunai with the addition of ventral and dorsal 20mm cannons.

Profile 40 – Nakajima J1N1-s MN 644 or 646, tail code 102, FPO2c Hareyama Fumio

This J1N1-s was photographed during a low-level raid during which it was destroyed at Lakunai on 18 October 1943. The airframe was only the second factory J1N1-s assigned to No. 251 *Ku*, often commanded by FPO2c Hareyama Fumio before he went missing on 21 October 1943 in another Irving.

Profile 41 – Nakajima L3Y1 Nell tail code U1-902

This Nell transport was photographed at Lakunai in mid-1943. Although it served with No. 251 *Ku* it was operated by the 11th Air Fleet.

No. 251 KOKUTAI
第251航空隊

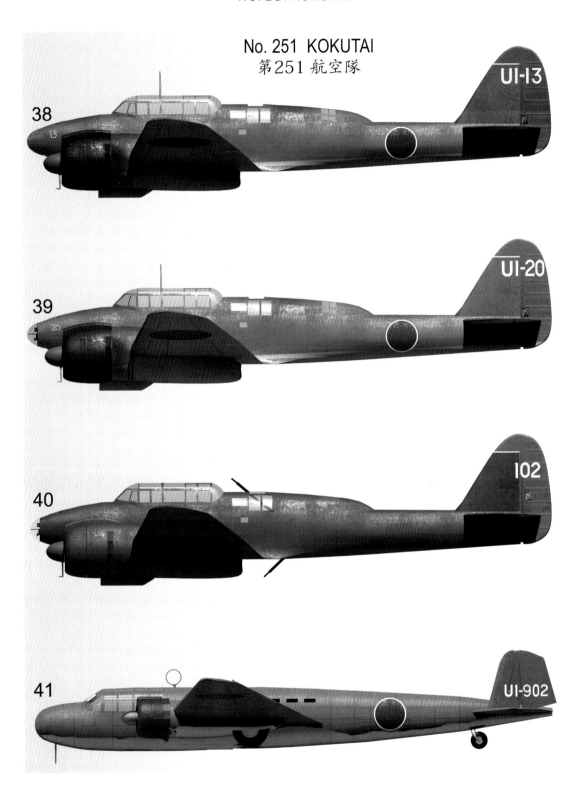

38

UI-13

39

UI-20

40

102

41

UI-902

Engineers adjust the cowl pushrods on a D4Y1 at Rabaul.

CHAPTER 11
No. 501 *Kokutai*

No. 501 *Ku* was the first Judy dive-bomber unit to see action in the South Seas, although the reconnaissance version of the type commenced service with No. 151 *Ku* in April 1943 (see Chapter 9). Activated on 1 July 1943, No. 501 *Ku*'s first echelon arrived at Rabaul on 19 October 1943 assigned to the 26th Air Flotilla, equipped with seven dive-bomber Judys.

The No. 501 *Ku* commanding officer throughout the unit's Rabaul sojourn was Captain Sakata Yoshito. Lieutenant Commander Inoue Fumito was appointed *hikotaicho* due to his experience in leading the first Val dive-bomber unit to the South Seas (No. 2 *Ku*) back in August 1942. Inoue subsequently spent time in Truk oversighting the developing concept of the Judy as a dive-bomber, leaving his deputy Lieutenant (jg) Odajima Hiro'o to lead No. 501 *Ku* missions from Rabaul when required. In this regard, five D4Y1-C Judys were sent to Truk in April 1943 to test out ordnance delivery including delivery of air-to-air phosphorous bombs. Airframe and powerplant adjustments were also established under tropical conditions.

No. 501 *Ku*'s first mission from Rabaul on 20 October 1943 also incurred the unit's first loss when a solitary Judy which departed just before dawn at 0500 failed to return. Over the next week it lost four more, including three to combat. When yet another Judy failed to return from a mission on 31 October this reduced the *kokutai* to just one airworthy aircraft. Accordingly the unit ceased operations for two weeks until 14 November when six replacements were flown down from Truk. Nonetheless combat losses continued steadily with more four Judys lost between November and February 1944. Although more replacements were delivered to Rabaul, due to limited production runs the *kokutai* never managed to field even a complete *chutai* of nine Judys. In fact, the largest mission No. 501 *Ku* ever flew from Rabaul comprised only five aircraft.

During the USN carrier raids against Rabaul in early November 1943, No. 501 *Ku*'s Judys dropped Type 3 air-to-air phosphorus bombs against the attacking Fifth Air Force B-25 strafers, with ineffective results. On such occasions, the type was commonly misidentified by Allied airmen as a JAAF Ki-61 Tony.

Although the Judys could deliver a solitary 250-kilogram bomb, the first mission carrying such did not occur until 24 November 1943. This was conducted by a single dive-bomber which ineffectively attacked USN destroyers *en route* to intercepting Japanese ships evacuating air personnel from Buka, Bougainville. The unit flew its last mission from Rabaul on 26 February 1944 after which the handful of remaining Judys were evacuated to Truk. The unit lost a total of nine Judys attributed to combat and several more to accidents. No. 501 *Ku* was deactivated on 10 July 1944, however it had all but ceased functioning by the time it left Rabaul at the end of February 1944.

Markings

The dive-bomber version of the D1Y1 was painted in dark green with grey undersurfaces. The unit prefix was "01" which represented the last two digits of No. 501 *Ku*. When the first echelon of seven Judys arrived at Rabaul on 19 October 1943 they were numbered 010 through to 070 (indicating numbers one to seven), with *shotaicho* aircraft being numbers 010, 040 and 070. It is unclear whether these numbers were replicated when airframes were lost, of whether they continued in sequence.

No. 501 Ku Judy tail code 01-070, as depicted in Profile 43, lies abandoned following combat damage at Cape Gloucester in late 1943.

No. 501 KOKUTAI
第501 航空隊

二式艦上偵察機
須賀 3193 號

Profile 42 – Yokosuka D4Y1 tail code 01-010, Lieutenant (jg) Odajima Hiro'o

Lieutenant (jg) Odajima Hiro'o served as *hikotaicho/chutaicho* of the No. 501 *Ku* Rabaul contingent, personally leading numerous missions. The twin stripes on the fin indicate his *chutaicho* status. Note the curved forward camouflage demarcation line.

Profile 43 – Yokosuka D4Y1 MN 3193, tail code 01-070

This airframe was abandoned at Cape Gloucester in late 1943. The airframe was examined by Allied intelligence after US Marines occupied the area in May 1944. During this inspection the tail was retrieved and taken to the US where it was displayed at Florence Air Museum in South Carolina until its closure in 1997. Note the illustrated Yokosuka manufacturing stencil as applied above the tail code which translates as "Type 2 ship-based reconnaissance aircraft, Yokosuka manufacturer's number 3193".

No. 552 KOKUTAI
第552航空隊

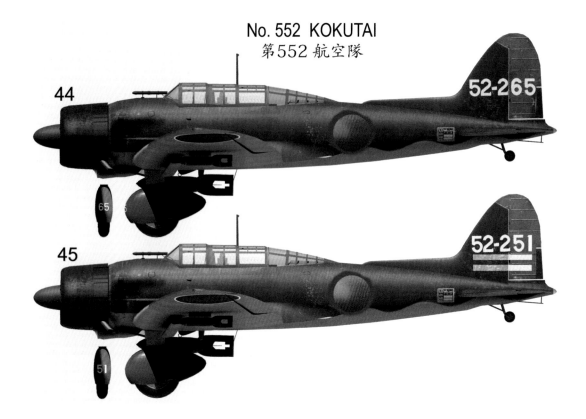

Profile 44 – D3A2 Model 22 MN 3571, tail code 52-265, Keravat, January 1944, pilot Flyer1c Hiramatsu Norihiko, observer FPO1c Hayashita Mitsuru

This Model 22 participated in the suite of dive-bombing missions from 17 to 31 December 1943 against Arawe (Cape Merkus) on West New Britain. It was lost in the early hours of 14 January 1944 after departing in the early morning with three other Vals for a night attack against US Marines on Mono Island. Led by *hikotaicho* Lieutenant (jg) Yamaguchi Tomojiro, each Val toted one 250-kilogram bomb, with an extra 60-kilogram bomb lugged by the fourth dive-bomber. Over the target at 0220 they were intercepted by radar-equipped F4U-2 Corsairs from VF(N)-75. FPO1c Hayashita Mitsuru's Val was shot up and later crashed into New Britain hills when trying to make home, either due to marginal conditions or an impaired airframe. The operations sheet notes that the wounded Hayashita was assisted by villagers to reach the coast from where an IJN launch returned him to Rabaul. The pilot Flyer1c Hiramatsu Norihiko was buried near the crash site by villagers.

Profile 45 – D3A2 Model 22 tail code 52-251, Kerevat, January 1944, *hikotaicho* pilot Lieutenant Hayashihara Moto'o

This Model 22 Val carries two horizontal tail stripes indicating Hayashihara's *chutaicho* status within No. 552 *Ku*.

CHAPTER 12
No. 552 *Kokutai*

No. 552 *Ku* was a unique Val unit as it specialised in night dive-bombing attacks. It entered the theatre late, only to come up against overwhelming odds which caused grievous losses, and thus the deployment lasted less than three months.

After receiving 25 new D3A2 Model 22 airframes at Truk, No. 552 *Ku* flew down to Kerevat, Rabaul, where it arrived over a three-day period commencing on 17 November 1943. A small detachment was sent to Kavieng the following week to attain theatre familiarisation and conduct anti-submarine patrols. The unit's first combat mission, a night shipping strike, was flown by a dozen Vals from Rabaul on 3 December 1943. One was shot down by anti-aircraft fire, and another was destroyed upon return with its gunner killed.

No. 552 *Ku* was withdrawn to Truk on 5 December 1943, where it undertook ten days training in night dive-bombing techniques. When news broke of the US landing at Arawe in New Britain, the unit was ordered back to Kerevat at short notice, arriving on 18 December with an inventory of around 25 airframes. Three days later it launched twenty Vals alongside ten more from No. 582 *Ku* on a morning attack against Cape Merkus. Although three No. 552 *Ku* Vals were shot down by USAAF Lightnings, they attacked the same target that same afternoon. This mission comprised a total of eighteen Vals, nine each from Nos. 552 and 582 *Ku*, with No. 552 *Ku* losing another dive-bomber to enemy fighters.

Both Val units pressed further attacks against shipping off Cape Merkus on 26, 27, 29 and 31 December, sustaining heavy losses. The 26 December mission in particular was severe, incurring a loss of eight of the thirteen participants. Meanwhile, back at Truk seven replacement Model 22s arrived from the No. 2 Air Arsenal at Yokosuka. These were ferried down to Kerevat in time to enter service at the end of 1943.

With its inventory depleted by the Cape Merkus campaign, No. 552 *Ku* now faced overpowering odds on nearly every mission, including attacks from night fighters. Following further losses, on 26 January 1944 the handful of surviving Vals were flown back to Truk from Kerevat where they operated until the end of February 1944. The *kokutai* was disbanded the following month.

Markings

The unit's Vals left the Aichi factory painted in overall dark green with grey undersides, and were allocated tail prefix "52" representing the last two digits of No. 552 *Ku*. The Vals were numbered 251 onwards, and painted the last two digits of the tail number on the forward wheel spat. The airframes left the Aichi factory with white piping around the *hinomaru* however this was painted over in the field for security reasons as illustrated.

No. 753 Ku Betty tail code 332, as illustrated in Profile 51, on its way to Guadalcanal.

Seen at Timor, T-351 carries two horizontal stripes to denote assignment to No. 2 Daitai. The square white background to the hinomaru and truncated tail gun position indicates a mid-1942 model Betty.

CHAPTER 13
Takao/No. 753 *Kokutai*

The Takao *Ku* was established on 1 April 1938 and first served in the China theatre equipped with Mitsubishi G3M2 Nells. It was re-equipped with the G4M1 Betty in 1940, thus becoming the first IJN unit to operate Mitsubishi's new bomber. From 15 November 1940 the Bettys were assigned the tail prefix "T" and the *kokutai* was re-assigned to the 23rd Air Flotilla on 14 July 1942 where it remained for the war's duration.

Following outbreak of the Pacific War, the unit advanced southwards to the Philippines and then to the Netherlands East Indies from where it conducted raids against northern Australia. Around mid-1942 the unit structured its flight operations into two *daitai* organised thus:

No. 1 *Daitai* (one horizontal stripe)

No. 1 *Buntai* (Nos. 11, 12 and 13 *Shotai*), T-301 to 315

No. 2 *Buntai* (Nos. 21, 22, 23 and 24 *Shotai*), T-316 to 330

No. 3 *Buntai* (Nos. 31, 32 and 33 *Shotai*), T-331 to 345

No. 2 *Daitai* (two horizontal stripes)

No. 4 *Buntai* (Nos. 41, 42 and 43 *Shotai*), T-346 to 360

No. 5 *Buntai* (Nos. 51, 52 and 53 *Shotai*), T-361 to 375

No. 6 *Buntai* (Nos. 61, 62 and 63 *Shotai*), T-376 to 390

Due to the growing pressures of the Guadalcanal campaign, on 23 September 1942 the Takao *Ku*'s No. 1 *Daitai* arrived in Rabaul with 27 Bettys. That afternoon it flew its first attack against Guadalcanal with a full *chutai* of nine bombers, and in subsequent weeks seven bombers were lost during the Solomons operations. On 1 October 1942, as part of the late 1942 IJN restructure, the unit was redesignated as No. 753 *Ku*. The Rabaul detachment returned to the NEI on 31 October 1942 where the unit's Bettys were given the new tail prefix "X1".

In September 1942 at least 62 Bettys were in service with the Takao *Ku*, and the following tail numbers were recorded: 301, 302, 303, 304, 305, 306, 307, 308, 311, 312, 314, 315, 316, 318, 329, 331, 332, 333, 334, 335, 336, 337, 339, 341, 343, 345 and 901 (the unit's Betty transport).

Markings

The unit underwent three markings regimes, and the administrative rebadging of the Takao *Ku* to No. 753 *Ku* occurred when the No. 1 *Daitai* was stationed at Rabaul. By December 1941 the group had established six *buntai* of Bettys all of which appeared in the factory "China Scheme" two-tone green and brown camouflage termed *kumogata* (cloud pattern). Nos. 1, 2, and 3 *Buntai/Chutai* Bettys are shown carrying an angled white (or yellow?) stripe along the fin leading edge at this time. The was later changed to a single or double horizontal fin stripe indicating Nos. 1 or 2 *Daitai*.

The Takao *Ku* (then No. 753 *Ku*) fell under the umbrella of the 23rd Air Flotilla on 14 July 1942 which was assigned to the South-Western Area Fleet. Accordingly, the tail code numbers were changed henceforth from white to red, with white piping applied to accentuate visibility as a field initiative. Although the new tail prefix "X2" was assigned it was never applied in the South Seas theatre due to security concerns. The one or two stripe system was maintained to indicate the respective *daitai*. Following the changeover to No. 753 *Ku*, the 23rd Air Flotilla association was identified by a red band around the fuselage.

Takao Ku Bettys T-315 and T-302 during their Rabaul deployment at Vunakanau. Both bombers are in "China Scheme" green and brown camouflage.

Betty tail code 321, as shown in Profile 53, on its way to Guadalcanal. The red tail code and red fuselage band are just visible in this black and white photo.

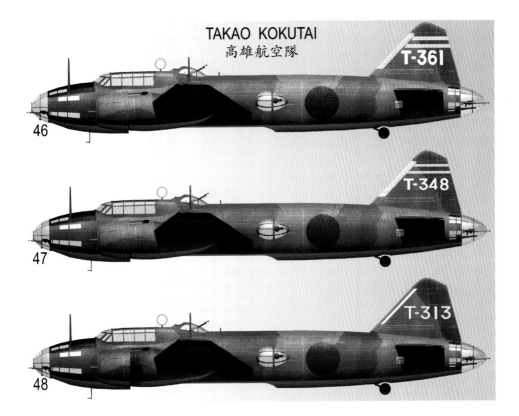

TAKAO KOKUTAI
高雄航空隊
T-361

T-348

T-313

46

47

48

Profile 46 – Mitsubishi G4M1 tail code T-361, No. 5 *Buntai*, shot down near Darwin 4 April 1942, aircraft commander Warrant Officer Ojino Takao

Three of six Takao *Ku* Bettys were shot down as they exited Darwin airspace following a raid on 4 April 1942, this bomber likely the one claimed by First Lieutenant John Landers flying a 9th Fighter Squadron Warhawk. The shattered wreckage was located by Australian soldiers the following day and six of the seven crew were initially buried on site. They were subsequently disinterred and reburied at the Japanese cemetery at Cowra, NSW, including aircraft commander Warrant Officer Ojino Takao. Parts of the wreckage were salvaged in the mid-1960s by the RAAF for display purposes.

Profile 47 – Mitsubishi G4M1 tail code T-348 (transferred to No. 4 *Ku* as F-348)

After serving in China, this bomber was transferred to No. 4 *Ku* in early February 1942. The *hikotaicho* of No. 4 *Ku*'s bomber wing was Lieutenant Commander Ito Takuzo, who flew the aircraft to Rabaul on 11 February 1942 with its new "F" prefix, along with Bettys F-350 (ex T-350) and F-354 (ex T-354). It was subsequently shot down during the calamitous 20 February 1942 attack against the carrier USS *Lexington*. The two stripes indicate the bomber's assignment to No. 2 *Daitai*. The bomber is illustrated as it appeared in January 1942 in the Philippines.

Profile 48 –Mitsubishi G4M1 tail code T-313, No. 1 *Buntai* (Rabaul detachment)

This Betty bore a thin white stripe just rear of the leading edge of the fin instead of covering the leading edge. It is illustrated as it appeared at Rabaul in September 1942.

TAKAO/ No. 753 KOKUTAI
高雄/ 第753 航空隊

T-317

49

T-305

50

332

51

T-339

52

321

53

Profile 49 – Mitsubishi G4M1 tail code T-317, No. 2 *Buntai* (Rabaul Detachment), shot down 28 September 1942, FPO2c Nogawa Itsuki

This Betty was one of four lost by the Takao *Ku* over Guadalcanal on 28 September 1942. The bomber formation that day comprised 27 Bettys, with a *chutai* each contributed by the Kanoya, Misawa and Takao *Ku*. Rather than approaching Guadalcanal directly, the formation leader Lieutenant Morita Rinji from the Misawa *Ku* instead negotiated Guadalcanal's west coast, subsequently turning left to approach Henderson Field from the southwest. The manoeuver permitted 34 intercepting Wildcats additional time to climb following an air raid warning. In a textbook interception, most Wildcat pilots were perfectly placed to mount attacks with the escorting Zeros out of position. The Takao *Ku* formation was hardest hit, losing four bombers including this one flown by FPO2c Nogawa Itsuki.

Profile 50 – Mitsubishi G4M1 tail code T-305, No. 1 *Buntai*, shot down Guadalcanal 27 September 1942, FPO1c Asato Matsuo

This Betty was one of nine Takao *Ku* bombers which attacked Guadalcanal on 27 September 1942, alongside another *chutai* from the Kisarazu *Ku* escorted by 38 Zeros. The formation was met by 35 Wildcats, but Major Kirk Armistead and Captain Marion Carl climbed the fastest and were the only ones to attack before the Zeros could intervene. These pilots claimed four Bettys downed, and likely accounted for T-305 and also a Kisarazu *Ku* Betty. Damage to two other bombers forced one to ditch in Rekata Bay, and another landed with one engine shot out at Buka.

Profile 51 – G4M1 Model 11, tail code 332, No. 3 *Buntai*

This bomber was photographed headed for Guadalcanal shortly after the transition to No. 753 *Ku*. The letter "T" was painted out and the tail markings reapplied in red with white piping. The bomber is painted in the China scheme and has a field-modified truncated rear gun position.

Profile 52 – G4M1 MN 3677, tail code T-339, observer Lieutenant (jg) Takanori Miyagi

On the early morning of 6 July 1943, 23 Bettys departed Koepang to attack Coomalie airfield, south of Darwin, which they bombed just before lunch. Two were shot down during combat with Darwin-based Spitfires. The wreckage of this bomber was later identified in a swamp 32 miles southwest of Batchelor airfield. The bodies of three of the eight aircrew were recovered and are today buried in Cowra Cemetery. The other Betty came down over ocean. Note that after analysis of the wreckage the "T" code was included in the intelligence report. This meant that either the bomber still retained its original Takao *Ku* prefix or perhaps an overlaying "X2" code had been burned away in the ensuring fire.

Profile 53 – G4M1 tail code 321, No. 2 *Buntai*

This bomber was also photographed headed for Guadalcanal shortly after the transition from the Takao *Ku* to No. 753 *Ku*. The prefix "X2" was not applied and in this case the tail number was applied without white piping. The bomber was photographed before a tail stripe had been applied.

This photo was taken during warm-up for No. 701 Ku's first mission from Vunakanau on the morning of 2 December 1942. Five Nells flew reconnaissance missions although all soon returned in capricious weather. Although by now serving as No. 701 Ku, Mihoro Ku markings are still present. G3M2 tail code M-341, the subject of Profile 54, is in the foreground.

The rear fuselage of G3M2 tail code 375, as illustrated in Profile 56, at Lae after the area was captured by Allied forces.

CHAPTER 14
Mihoro/No. 701 *Kokutai*

The Mihoro *Ku* (sometimes pronounced "Bihoro") first served in the French Indochina and China theatres. The *kokutai* was in the Marshall Islands during the late 1942 IJN restructure, when it was redesignated No. 701 *Ku* on 1 November and called forward to Vunakanau despite being still equipped with antiquated G3M2 Nells. It arrived there on 1 December with commanding officer Captain Yamada Yutaka and *hikocho* Lieutenant Commander Higai Joji. Higai was a prestigious IJN veteran of the land attack corps who had previously served as the *hikotaicho* of the Kasumigaura *Ku*, a unit steeped in IJN tradition.

No. 701 *Ku* moved to Rabaul to fill the gap caused by the departure of No. 4 *Ku* whose few survivors had been recalled to Japan in late September 1942 (see Chapter 5). During interludes at Rabaul, Higai focused his crews on night torpedo attack training. The No. 4 *Buntai* first flew sector searches from Rabaul on 2 December, before on 6 December 1942 it conducted its first bombing mission in the South Seas. This was against Buna with sixteen Nells of Nos. 5 and 6 *Buntai* led by *hikotaicho* Lieutenant Iwaya Fumio. The following day the attack was repeated, this time with eighteen Nells from Nos. 4, 5 and 6 *Buntai*. On 17 December nine No. 701 *Ku* Nells set out to conduct a night raid over Port Moresby. Split into three groups, they became lost due to bad weather. On 24 December seven of the unit's Nells again headed for Port Moresby. Unusually, among the usual bomb load, one bomber also carried a single 800-kilogram bomb. However, the mission was again thwarted by bad weather, and they bombed Buna instead.

Lieutenant Iwaya Fumio supervised Nell operations as *hikotaicho*. No. 701 *Ku* was a key player when the cruiser USS *Chicago* was lost to a series of aircraft-delivered torpedo attacks throughout the early hours of 29-30 January 1943. Rabaul determined that approaching USN warships threatened Operation *Ke*, the evacuation of Guadalcanal. Accordingly, a combined strike force of 32 Bettys and Nells, furnished by Nos. 701 and 705 *Ku*, left Vunakanau on the afternoon of 29 January 1943. At 1920 sixteen No. 705 *Ku* Bettys opened the attack with a long torpedo approach, followed by *hikocho* Higai leading No. 701 *Ku*'s No. 1 *Chutai*. After an initial Nell was downed by retaliatory anti-aircraft fire, Higai's Nell was splashed three minutes later. Three trailing Nells were also hit and were forced to make precautionary landings at Buin and Buka.

However, the attack had been successful, and the *Chicago* sank the next morning. Some weeks later in late February 1943 No. 701 *Ku* left the theatre. It lost a total of sixteen Nells to combat in the South Seas, with a handful also lost to accidents.

Markings

Whilst the Mihoro *Ku* did not serve in the South Seas *per se*, No. 701 *Ku* Nells still carried Mihoro *Ku* markings which they retained for the first few weeks of operations at Rabaul. Several older bombers still retained the brown and green "China scheme" camouflage, however replacement airframes arriving from early January 1943 onwards were in overall green. Similar to the Genzan *Ku*, the double fuselage band indicates the Mihoro *Ku*'s assignment to the 22nd Air Flotilla. Associated tail code ranges and *buntai* markings were thus:

No. 1 *Buntai*, M-311 to 325 (single horizontal fin stripe)

No. 2 *Buntai* M-331 to 345 (single horizontal with one vertical fin stripe)

No. 3 *Buntai* M-351 to 365 (double horizontal fin stripe)

No. 4 *Buntai* M-371 to 383 (single horizontal thick fin stripe)

Similar to the Genzan *Ku* Nells, the legacy code system stemmed from the China era and was unique as the second numeral indicated the assigned *shotai* and the last the sequential number of the aircraft within that *shotai*. Thus, tail code 363 indicated the third bomber assigned to the No. 6 *Shotai*. The normal *shotai* complement was three aircraft, however sometimes a fourth or even fifth served as a reserve aircraft and was numbered accordingly. This system departed from the norm of later land-attack units which allocated sequential numerical sequences to each *buntai*.

Sometimes a white or yellow leading edge was painted on the fins, a warning marker for the dorsal gunner to avoid the fin during defensive fire. When the Mihoro *Ku* was redesignated as No. 701 *Ku* the unit was allocated the prefix "Y1". However, this code was never implemented at Rabaul for security reasons. Instead, the previous "M" prefix was painted out, leaving the three-digit identifier to stand alone. When No. 701 *Ku* was decommissioned on 15 March 1943, its prefix "Y1" was reassigned to No. 755 *Ku*.

Profile 54 – Nakajima G3M2 tail code M-341, No. 2 *Buntai*

This No. 701 *Ku* Nell was the first bomber in No. 4 *Shotai* and was photographed at Rabaul on 2 December 1942. It is illustrated carrying eight 60-kilogram bombs and with a yellow leading edge marker on the fin. The "China scheme" camouflage is badly worn.

Profile 55 – Nakajima G3M2 tail code M-371, No. 4 *Buntai*

This Nell was the first bomber in No. 7 *Shotai* and is illustrated carrying a solitary 800-kilogram bomb.

Profile 56 – Nakajima G3M2 MN 6346, tail code 325, No. 1 *Buntai*

This No. 701 *Ku* Nell was painted overall green and was abandoned at Lae after a landing mishap around January 1943. It is illustrated carrying two 250-kilogram bombs.

Profile 57 – Nakajima G3M2 tail code M-355, No. 3 *Buntai*

This G3M2 showcases the double horizontal fin stripe of No. 701 *Ku*'s No. 3 *Buntai*.

MIHORO/ 701 KOKUTAI
美幌/ 701 航空隊

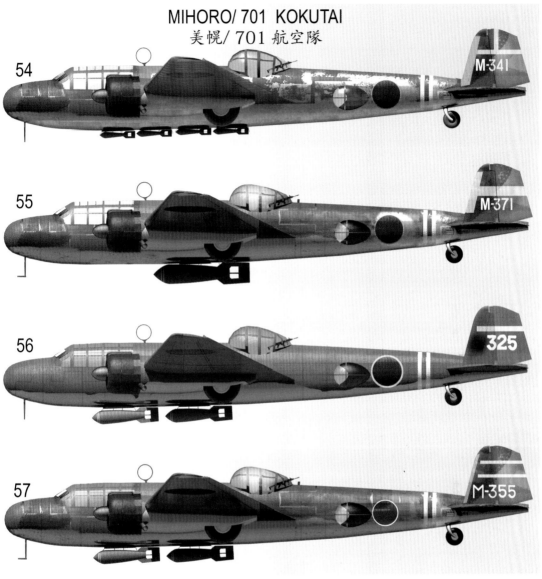

54 M-341

55 M-371

56 325

57 M-355

Double horizontal stripes on these Nells showcase No. 701 Ku's No. 3 Buntai, although the wartime censor has removed all tail codes.

In the foreground of this Genzan Ku formation is G3M2 tail code G-351, as illustrated in Profile 59, showcasing its topside diagonal chutaicho wing markings.

Genzan Ku Nell G-374, as depicted in Profile 60, displays the heavy weathering of its paint scheme somewhere over the South Seas.

CHAPTER 15
Genzan *Kokutai*

The word "Genzan" is a legacy name located in the Korean Peninsula and was the Japanese pronunciation from the era when Korea was a Japanese colony. It is today pronounced "Wonsan" in Korean, sometimes mistranslated that way from Japanese wartime documents. Although the Genzan *Ku* was established in Korea, when the Pacific War broke out it was based at Tan Son Nhat airfield outside Saigon in Indochina, serving under the 22nd Air Flotilla. It was called forward to Rabaul on 20 April 1942 with an advance *chutai* of nine G3M2 Nells, flown in from Truk led by Lieutenant Nakanishi Tsugikazu. In preparation for its South Seas deployment, the unit had trained in Truk since 6 April. The first task of the "Nakanishi detachment" was to take over Rabaul's surveillance flight regime then being undertaken by No. 4 *Ku* Bettys. This allowed these Bettys to resume offensive operations against Port Moresby.

The unit's commanding officer was Captain Yamashita Sakae, and on 27 April, two more *chutai* of Nells arrived at Vunakanau. As the performance and flying characteristics of the Nell differed substantially from the Betty, the two types usually flew separately when conducting joint missions.

By the end of April 1942, the unit based itself at Vunakanau in preparation to support Operation *MO*, the invasion of Port Moresby. The Genzan *Ku* was to be deployed as high-level bombers, and around midday on 7 May 1942 Allied warships were bombed by nineteen Nells loaded with 250-kilogram bombs. Four days later a concerted effort with separate raids by the Genzan *Ku* and No. 4 *Ku* was flown against Allied shipping, but without success. Following the failure of Operation *MO*, the unit continued bombing missions against Port Moresby, with its last mission on 29 June 1942 after which it departed the theatre. Under the IJN restructure on 1 November 1942 the unit was redesignated as No. 755 *Ku*, with the unit prefix "G" replaced by "Y2".

Perhaps surprisingly the Genzan *Ku* lost only one aircraft during its Rabaul deployment. This was a Nell which was written off at Vunakanau on 26 June 1942 after landing with severe combat damage and three crewmen badly wounded.

Markings

The Genzan *Ku* inventory comprised early model G3M2s in "China scheme" two-tone camouflage. A double white fuselage band indicated assignment to the 22nd Air Flotilla. Tail code ranges and *buntai* markings were thus:

No. 1 *Buntai*, G-311 to 324 (single oblique fin stripe)

No. 2 *Buntai* G-331 to 354 (double oblique fin stripe)

No. 3 *Buntai* G-361 to 374 (single oblique thick fin stripe)

No. 4 *Buntai* G-381 to 394 (single stripe with right-angle intersection)

The *buntai/shotai* indicator code system stemmed from the China era and was similar to that used by the Mihoro/No. 701 *Ku* (see Chapter 14). This was unique insofar as the second digit indicated the *shotai* number and the last the number of the aircraft assigned to that *shotai*. Thus, tail code 374 indicated the fourth bomber assigned to No. 7 *Shotai*. The normal complement for a *shotai* was three aircraft, however, sometimes more were added as reserves and numbered accordingly. *Chutaicho* aircraft were marked by diagonal wing markings just behind the engine.

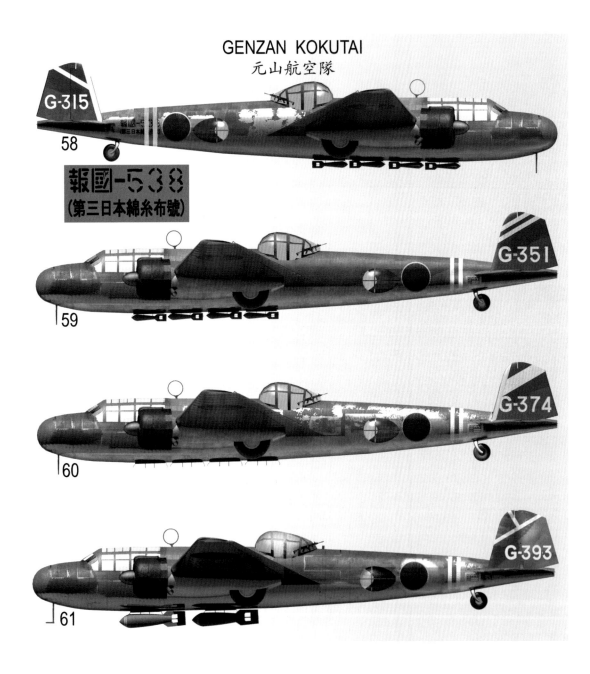

GENZAN KOKUTAI

元山航空隊

Profile 58 – Nakajima G3M2 MN 460, tail code G-315, *hokoku* HK-538, No. 1 *Buntai*

This No. 1 *Buntai* Nell was abandoned at Lae and examined by Allied Intelligence in September 1943 after the area was recaptured by Australian troops. The *hokoku* marking indicates it was the third airframe donated by the Yard Cloth Export Association of Japan based in Osaka, and it had been dedicated and blessed at Osaka Airport on Sunday 16 November 1941.

Profile 59 – Nakajima G3M2 tail code G-351, No. 2 *Buntai*

The double oblique fin stripe of this Genzan *Ku* G3M2 identifies its association with No. 2 *Buntai*. The bomber also had diagonal wing markings just behind the engine indicating a *chutaicho* aircraft.

Profile 60 – Nakajima G3M2 tail code G-374, No. 3 *Buntai*

The "China scheme" camouflage on this Genzan *Ku* Nell is badly worn. It is illustrated with empty bomb racks mounted under fuselage.

Profile 61 – Nakajima G3M2 tail code G-393, No. 4 *Buntai*

This Genzan *Ku* Nell is illustrated toting two 250-kilogram bombs. It displays the single stripe with a right-angled intersection indicating service with No. 4 *Buntai*.

A Genzan Ku No. 4 Buntai bomber with tail code censored, airborne over Indochina circa 1941.

Greater Japan Airways Kawanishi H6K2-L civilian registration J-BGOE, as depicted in Profile 62, on a slipway.

CHAPTER 16
GREATER JAPAN AIRWAYS

With additional resources demanded by the China theatre, the civilian national flag carrier Japan Air Transport was called upon to move troops and materiel. Accordingly in December 1938 Japan's military government created a monopoly airline through acquisition of a half-share of Japan Air Transport which they named Greater Japan Airlines (*Dai Nippon Koku Kabushiki Kaisha*). It was headquartered at Haneda airport and divided into two wings, one each for the Japanese Army and Japanese Navy. Throughout the war its aircraft retained civilian registrations.

In early 1942 Greater Japan Airlines commenced scheduled runs to Rabaul and other Pacific locations, however South Seas services became almost non-existent by mid-1942 when the IJN decided instead to operate Combined Fleet flying boats to front-line locations. Nonetheless, by 1943 the airline had instituted regular services from Taiwan throughout the Philippines, Netherlands East Indies, Singapore, Thailand and southern China. The airline's operations continued until Japan's surrender in August 1945. When Haneda airport came under the control of US forces the following month the airline was disbanded.

For its Pacific and overseas routes, the airline operated a fleet of twenty-three H6K2-L and H6K4-L transport versions of the Mavis. Although not military aircraft *per se*, and constructed without defensive blisters or guns, these flying boats were contracted by the IJN primarily to transport VIP military personnel and urgent supplies into the South Seas, including occasional visits to New Guinea ports and Rabaul. They often returned carrying returning VIPs, more serious medical evacuees and documents including unit records. The civilian status of these aircraft did not prevent them from being shot down. At least two civilian Mavises were downed in combat engagements. One of these incidents is outlined in Profile 63, while on 28 December 1944 a VPB-104 Privateer shot down another Mavis transport over the South China Sea.

Markings

The Greater Japan Airlines Mavises initially served in pre-war NMF, with protective marine inhibitor gloss applied to the hull, however as the war progressed they were painted in IJN green. Each initially retained a capital letter "J" on the fin as the prefix of the civilian registration followed by four *romanji* letters on the hull as the civilian registration. The initial inventory was named after meteorological phenomena, shrines, cities or seas around Japan. These names were painted in *kanji* on the forward hull in black, underneath the airline's logo. Photos of a Greater Japan Airlines Mavis visiting Rabaul in early 1942 show it without civilian registration markings, however it is unclear whether this was the work of the wartime censor, or whether the markings were removed *per se*.

Below is the complete list of registrations of all Mavis transports used by Greater Japan Airlines during the war, along with their names in *kanji* where known:

J-BEAM, J-BFOR, J-BFOS *Asashio* 朝潮 (Morning Tide), J-BFOT *Akebono* 明保野, J-BFOX, J-BFOY, J-BFOZ, J-BGOB, J-BGOC *Hato*, J-BGOD, J-BGOE *Makigumo* 巻雲, J-BGOF, J-BGOG *Shinonome* 東雲, J-BGOH *Asanagi* 朝凪 J-BGOI *Yunagi* 柚凪, J-BGOJ *Oshioi*, J-BGOK *Akatsuki* 暁暁 (Shining Dawn), J-BGOL *Ariake* 有明, J-BPOA *Kozu* 公図 (Cadastral Map), J-BPOB *Mikura*, J-BPOC, J-BPOD and J-BPOE.

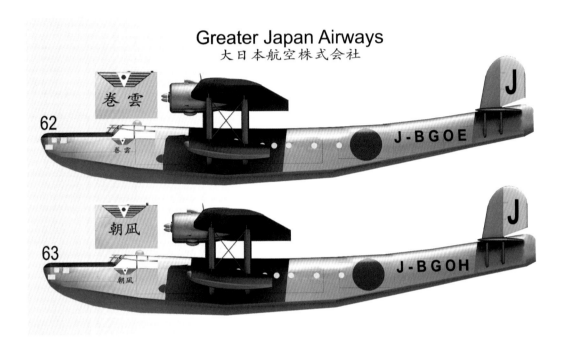

Profile 62 – Kawanishi H6K2-L J-BGOE *Makigumo* 巻雲

This Greater Japan Airlines flying boat is illustrated in its pre-war civilian markings. It was named *Makigumo* (Cirrus Cloud).

Profile 63 –Kawanishi H6K2-L J-BGOH *Asanagi* 朝凪

This Greater Japan Airlines Mavis named *Asanagi* (Morning Calm) departed Palau on 13 April 1944. Some hours later it was shot down north of New Guinea by a VB-106 PB4Y-2 Privateer. The contact report mistakenly described the aircraft as having a colour scheme of overall "purplish grey". The flying boat is illustrated in pre-war civilian markings.

Greater Japan Airlines Mavis J-BFOZ at anchor in early 1942. The location is unknown.

A Greater Japan Airlines H6K2-L moored in Rabaul harbour in early 1942. It is unclear whether the registration and tail markings have been removed by the censor, or whether they were painted over for security reasons.

TAINAN KOKUTAI
台南航空隊

Profile 64 – Nakajima J1N1-c MN 15, tail code V-1

This Irving was one of the first three reconnaissance J1N1-c Type 2 Land Reconnaissance aircraft to become operational in the South Seas. These were first deployed to Rabaul in July 1942, and were later briefly based at Lae. The fuselage *hinomaru* had a white border and the "V" and "1" were disproportionate in size.

Profile 65 – Mitsubishi C5M2 Babs tail code V-4

The Tainan *Ku* C5M2s wore a factory applied light olive brown scheme. A black tail code was reapplied over the original ones of white with red piping, which dated back to when the unit was in Bali in early 1942.

Profile 66 – Mitsubishi G6M1-L2 MN 209, tail code V-903

This Betty previously served with No. 1 *Ku* as tail code Z-985 (see Profile 3), having left the Mitsubishi factory in the two-tone "China scheme" as a G6M1-L experimental gunship. The gunship concept was not implemented, however, and the gap in the lower fuselage is the space from where a defensive gondola was removed. The bomber's first tail number was 181 from its experimental days as a gunship, then it became Z-985 with No. 1 *Ku* before finally becoming V-903 with the Tainan *Ku* as illustrated there.

CHAPTER 17
Tainan *Kokutai*

The Tainan *Ku* was primarily a Zero fighter unit, and its complex markings are covered in *Pacific Profiles Volume Five.* In addition to its fighter inventory, it was assigned several C5M2 Babs, three J1N1-c Irving reconnaissance twins and three transport Bettys. The Irvings were on the leading edge of Japanese aircraft design and were being trialed by the Tainan *Ku* in the South Seas after arriving in Rabaul in July 1942. The Babs was used for long-range reconnaissance including over targets as distant as Horn Island (Australia), and numerous parts of the Solomons. They became a key platform in the provision of weather reports during the Guadalcanal campaign.

Meanwhile, following the loss of the first Irving to Airacobras on 2 August 1942, the two remaining twins were deployed judiciously, mainly in the Solomons. These experimental types were hampered at times from lack of spare parts and maintenance difficulties. Following the loss of the first Irving they undertook only three more missions in August 1942, five in September and then three in October. When the Japanese shifted focus to Guadalcanal from early August 1942, they ensured that both remaining J1N1-c Irvings remained Rabaul-based, and for the two successive days after the US invasion, these flew reconnaissance missions over the contested island. In the 1 November 1942 IJN restructure, the Tainan *Ku* became No. 251 *Ku*. The sole surviving J1N1-c from the original trio was flown back to Japan a few days later by Warrant Officer Ono Satoru. Following further evaluation of the type in Japan, the Irving was converted into an effective night-fighter, largely as a result of the trials with the Tainan *Ku* which played an instrumental role in its development.

Back in Japan, former Tainan *Ku* pilots FCPO Kudo Shigetoshi and Warrant Officer Ono Satoru pushed authorities in the Japanese Department of Navy to develop the Irving as a night fighter, an aircraft they knew well from their time in Rabaul. Whilst No. 251 *Ku* returned to the South Seas with Zeros in May 1943 (see Chapter 10), on 1 September 1943 it was reclassified exclusively as a night-fighter unit using Nakajima's new version of the Irving, the J1N1-s.

The tail of Tainan Ku Betty V-903, as depicted in Profile 66, lies wrecked on the ground after being targeted by Allied air attack at Buna.

Southeast Area Fleet Transport Detachment G6M1-L tail code P-911, as shown in Profile 73, lies in the background while curious Americans inspect other wreckage at Lae following its recapture in September 1943.

Against the backdrop of Tavurvur volcano near Rabaul, an idling IJN crew await their passengers at Lakunai airfield in late 1943. This G4M1 transport has the No. 1001 Ku tail prefix "ヨ A".

CHAPTER 18
Fleet Transports & Miscellaneous

A variety of land-based transports and flying boats served the logistical needs of the South Seas combat units, and technical units also visited the area to conduct field trials and research. Although combat units were assigned transport aircraft, their control fell under the umbrella of the 11th Air Fleet or other fleet commands in order to coordinate logistical requirements. Nonetheless, these carried the tail prefix of the unit with which they predominantly served.

H6K4 Mavis tail code P-922, as depicted in Profile 76, moored at Rabaul.

G6M1-L tail code GF-2, as illustrated in Profile 68, in Japan.

FLEET Transports & Miscellaneous
輸送機連合艦隊の

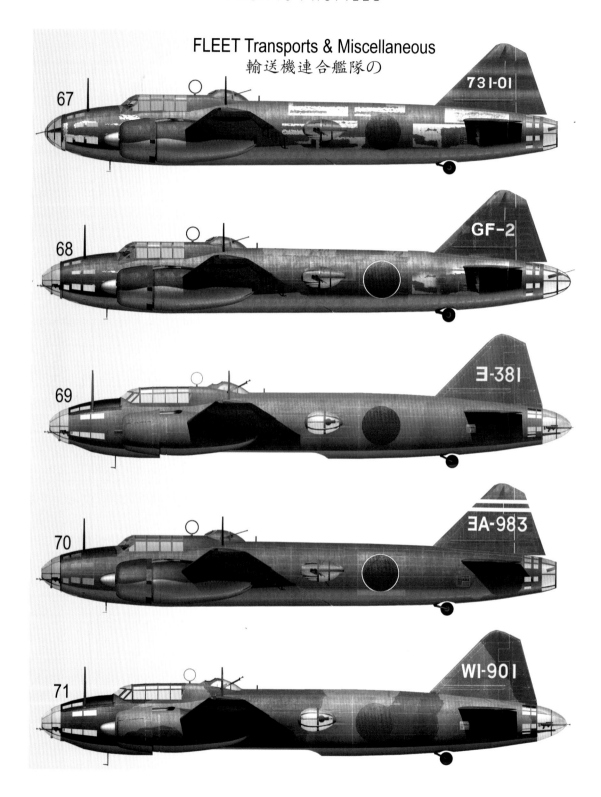

67

68

69

70

71

Profile 67 – G4M1 tail code 731-01, 11ᵗʰ Air Fleet Transport Detachment

This Betty was photographed visiting Rabaul in November 1943. The heavy weathering on the airframe suggests it was transferred as war-weary from an unidentified previous combat unit. The prefix "731" was the allocated prefix for the 11ᵗʰ Air Fleet Transport Detachment later in the war.

Profile 68 – G6M1-L tail code GF-2, Combined Fleet Transport Detachment

Combined Fleet transports infrequently visited the South Seas theatre, usually for the purpose of carrying VIPs. "GF" was the prefix allocated to the detachment.

Profile 69 – G4M1 tail code ∃-381, Yokosuka Naval Technical Department

This Betty was one of two maintained by the Yokosuka *Ku* but assigned to the Yokosuka Naval Technical Department which visited Rabaul in April 1942. These Bettys had the *katakana* tail prefix "∃" (*yo*), similar to a capital "E" backwards. The pair brought civilian engineers to Rabaul to undertake technical research, including the effects on performance due to high humidity and the effect on engines resulting from the ingestion of volcanic dust.

Profile 70 – G4M1 tail code ∃A-983, No. 1001 *Ku*, Kavieng early 1944

In July 1943 additional *kokutai* were established at Yokosuka with a series of tail codes which included the *katakana* "∃" followed by a sequential Roman letter. First established was No. 1001 *Ku*, a specialist transport unit, given the tail code prefix "∃A". The next three sequential codes were issued to new *kokutai* by way of example, none of which served in the South Seas. These were "∃B" (No. 503 *Ku* established on 1 October 1943), "∃C" (No. 301 *Ku* 5 November 1943) and "∃D" (No. 302 *Ku* 1 March 1944).

Profile 71 – G4M1 tail code W1-901, No. 201 *Ku* (managed by 11ᵗʰ Air Fleet)

No. 201 *Ku* was a Zero fighter unit assigned to the 24ᵗʰ Air Flotilla with the tail prefix "W1". By mid-July 1943 about half the unit was sent to Buin with 25 Zeros, however on 8 October 1943, No. 204 *Ku* was withdrawn from Bougainville operations leaving No. 201 *Ku* as the only defender of Buin. However, within a few weeks Buin was declared unsuitable for fighter operations, and the base was effectively vacated by all aerial units, leaving behind only reduced garrisons. During this period W1-901 was kept busy with the withdrawal of key equipment and personnel back to Rabaul. Note that although an early model Betty, it had a spinner fitted.

FLEET Transports & Miscellaneous
輸送機連合艦隊の

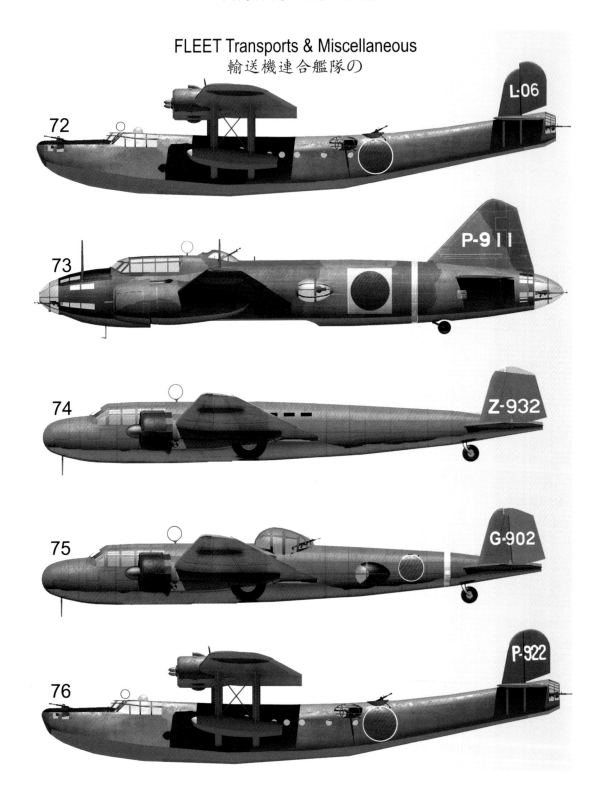

72

L-06

73

P-911

74

Z-932

75

G-902

76

P-922

Profile 72 – Kawanishi H6K4 Mavis, tail code L-06, 4th Fleet Transport Section

On 26 June 1942 Australian scouts carefully surveyed the small coastal outpost of Salamaua, New Guinea, in the lead-up to a commando attack against the area. Just after lunch one recorded the tail code of this Mavis as it disgorged eleven men and personal gear ashore, including suitcases, duffle bags and a ceremonial box covered with white cloth. This was carried from the flying boat to the wharf, then on to the local commander's house.

Profile 73 – G6M1-L MN 714, tail code P-911, Southeast Area Fleet Transport Detachment

This transport was abandoned at Lae following damage inflicted by an Allied air raid. It is an early model airframe with two-tone brown and green camouflage but has subsequently had a white square background to the *hinomaru* applied in the field.

Profile 74 – Yokosuka L3Y2 tail code Z-932, No. 1 *Ku*, operated by 11th Air Fleet

This transport version of the Nell served with No. 1 *Ku* and had no gondola, small windows along the rear fuselage and was painted overall green. It was photographed at Vunakanau in March 1942.

Profile 75 – Mitsubishi G3M2 tail code G-902, Genzan *Ku*, 11th Air Fleet Transport Detachment

This Nell was seen at Kavieng in May 1942, and was operated by the Genzan *Ku* primarily to assist the unit's movement to Rabaul from Truk.

Profile 76 – Kawanishi H6K4 Mavis tail code P-922, Southeast Area Fleet Transport Detachment

This Mavis was photographed anchored at the Malaguna seaplane base, Rabaul, in late 1942.

G4M1 tail code 731-01, the subject of Profile 67, parked at Lakunai in November 1943.

No. 705 Ku's No. 2 Buntai heading home to Vunakanau, on return from Guadalcanal. Ships can be seen at anchor in Rabaul harbour in the background.

Misawa Ku G4M H-351 carries a split vertical tail band of No. 3 Buntai.

CHAPTER 19
Misawa/No. 705 *Kokutai*

The Misawa *Ku* was formed on 10 February 1942 as a G4M1 Betty bomber unit. It was assigned to the 26th Air Flotilla with the tail prefix "H". After training in Japan, it moved to Saipan before being called forward to Rabaul in August 1942. The unit was initially created with three *buntai*, then became No. 705 *Ku* on 1 November 1942 during the late 1942 IJN restructure. At the end of December 1942 unit strength was increased to four *buntai* when an additional *buntai* was assimilated from the disbanded No. 707 *Ku*. The commanding officer at establishment was Captain Sugawara Masao who was replaced during the restructure by Captain Konishi Yasuo, after which the *kokutai* became known as the "Konishi Unit". Konishi remained as commanding officer until No. 705 *Ku* was disbanded in May 1944.

The unit operated the most famous Betty of all, tail number 323, which was shot down on 18 April 1943 with commander of the Combined Fleet, Admiral Yamamoto Isoroku, aboard (see Profile 82).

The *kokutai* suffered horrendous losses, first in its guise as the Misawa *Ku* losing 30 Bettys to combat and accidents in the three-month period from August to October 1942. This was followed by a further 47 Bettys lost by No. 705 *Ku*. The last Betty loss took place during a night nuisance raid to Guadalcanal on 14 August 1943 flown by Lieutenant Yamasaki Tatsuya.

Markings

First, most Misawa *Ku* bombers carried one white fuselage stripe to denote assignment to the 26th Air Flotilla, although for unknown reasons sometimes it was not applied. This unit's complex markings system has been confused due to its three distinct markings regimes, the original being:

> No. 1 *Buntai*, tail range H-301 to 319, white fin tip

> No. 2 *Buntai* tail range H-320 to 339, one broad horizontal white band on fin

> No. 3 *Buntai* tail range H-340 to 369 one broad vertical band on fin

Following the late 1942 IJN restructure, No. 705 *Ku* was allocated new prefix "T1". No photograph exists to show this was ever applied, although the operations log shows replacement aircraft were initially allocated the "T1" prefix before leaving Japan. It thus appears these were painted out when they arrived at Rabaul for security reasons. When the fourth *buntai* was added at the end of December 1942 (acquired from the disbanded No. 707 *Ku*), the unit underwent a transitionary markings period. The commanding officer Captain Konishi Yasuo then authorised a new markings regime which was implemented in January 1943:

> No. 1 *Buntai*, tail codes 301 to 319, white fin tip removed

> No. 2 *Buntai* became No. 5 *Buntai*, tail codes 320 to 339, one narrow split white band on fin

No. 3 *Buntai* became No. 2 *Buntai* tail codes 340 to 369 one split (medium width) horizontal band on fin, sometimes yellow

No. 4 *Buntai* (from No. 707 *Ku*), tail codes 370 to 399 was renumbered No. 6 *Buntai*, one split broad vertical band on fin

In conjunction with the above, note that some airframes in between this changeover kept their extant markings regime, an example being as per Profile 89. Note also that the above tail numbers were replaced when one was lost, and like other Betty units, most allocated sequences were rarely filled. For example, the highest logged number in No. 4 *Buntai* is 383.

Profile 77 – Mitsubishi G4M1 Model 11 MN 1365, tail code H-352, No. 3 *Buntai*, ditched 10 September 1942, Lieutenant I'idzika Yutaka

Assigned to No. 3 *Buntai*, this early G4M1 airframe in the green and brown "China scheme" was transferred from No .3 *Buntai* of No. 4 *Ku* in September 1942 with the previous tail code F-353 series with two fin stripes. The bomber was flown by Lieutenant I'idzika Yutaka which was shot up by a VMF-223 Wildcat over Guadalcanal on 10 September 1942. With seven crew, I'idzika ditched the bomber in one fathom of water off New Georgia's coast due to fuel exhaustion resulting from pierced fuel tanks. The crew was confronted by a native police patrol the next day which shot I'idzika as he tried to escape. The other six crewmen were handed over to a coastwatcher the following day, and on 20 December were flown to Tulagi by PBY. They were then transferred to New Caledonia where they became POWs. Following the US occupation of New Georgia, this bomber was disassembled and salvaged by the Allied Technical Intelligence Unit.

Profile 78 – Mitsubishi G4M1 Model 11, tail code H-311, No. 1 *Buntai*

Assigned to the Misawa *Ku*'s No. 1 *Buntai*, unusually this airframe had a yellow leading edge on the fin and was one of the first overall-green Bettys to be assigned to the unit. It was photographed returning from a Guadalcanal mission in September 1942.

Profile 79 – Mitsubishi G4M1 Model 11, tail code H-362, No. 3 *Buntai*

This Misawa *Ku* Betty had a white narrow leading edge on the fin and was also photographed returning from a Guadalcanal mission in September 1942.

Profile 80 – Mitsubishi G4M1 Model 11, tail code H-323, No. 2 *Buntai*

This Misawa *Ku* Betty served during the late 1942 Guadalcanal campaign and appeared with a curved camouflage line, however it lacked the white fuselage band denoting the 26th Air Flotilla.

Profile 81 – Mitsubishi G4M1 Model 11, tail code H-383, No. 4 *Buntai*

This Betty carries hybrid markings. It was an original renumbered Model 11 airframe caught between the transition from the Misawa *Ku* to No. 705 *Ku*. Its first two numerals of "383" are larger than the final numeral 3, indicating it was renumbered around November 1942 as a reassigned member of No. 4 *Buntai*, but initially retaining the Misawa *Ku* prefix "H". It was photographed returning from a Guadalcanal mission in November 1942.

MISAWA KOKUTAI
三澤航空隊

77 H·352

78 H·311

79 H·362

80 H·323

81 H·383

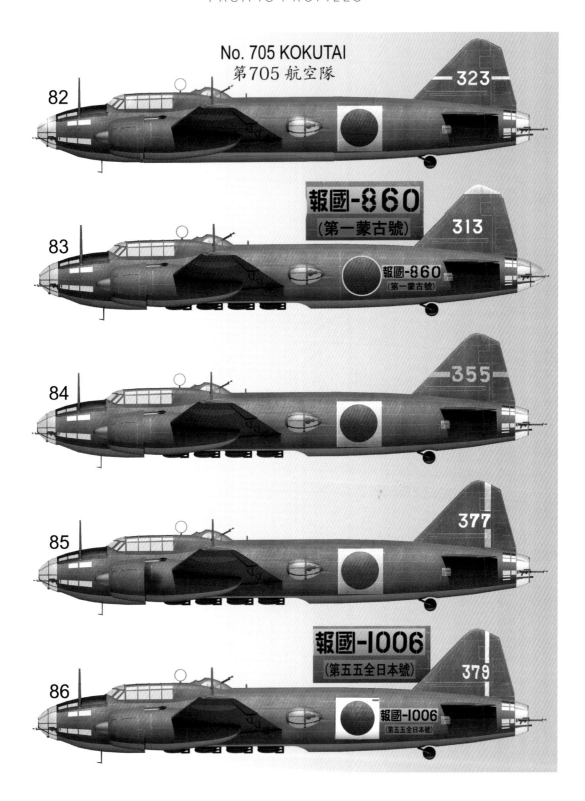

No. 705 KOKUTAI
第705航空隊

82   323

83   報國-860
      (第一蒙古號)
      313
      報國-860
      (第一蒙古號)

84   355

85   377

86   報國-1006
      (第五五全日本號)
      379
      報國-1006
      (第五五全日本號)

Profile 82 – Mitsubishi G4M1 Model 11 MN 2656, tail code 323, shot down 18 April 1943, pilot FCPO Kotani Takashi

The most famous Betty of all, this No. 705 *Ku* bomber was carrying Admiral Yamamoto Isoroku when it was shot down on 18 April 1943 by USAAF Lightnings. The bomber was almost brand new, a numerical replacement for H-323 (see Profile 80). The markings of this bomber have been consistently misrepresented over the years. It was administratively assigned to the No. 5 *Buntai*, and accordingly had a narrow white split stripe across the fin, confirmed from post-war photos taken at the site, along with a white square surrounding the fuselage *hinomaru*.

Profile 83 – Mitsubishi G4M1 Model 11 MN 1350, tail code 313 (previous 377), *hokoku* HK-860 第一蒙古號 (first Mongolia) shot down Guadalcanal early 1943

This bomber was formally dedicated as a *hokoku* patriotic donation in October 1942 at the Mengjiang Shrine in Hebei Province. The nature of the Mongolia donation stems from when the Mengjiang United Autonomous Government was renamed in August 1941 as the Mongolian Autonomous Federation. The bomber was initially assigned to No. 705 *Ku* with the tail code 377, but was reassigned to No. 1 *Buntai* around February 1943, and later replaced by another "377" (see Profile 85). It was shot down near Henderson Field on an unknown date not long afterwards.

Profile 84 – Mitsubishi G4M1 Model 11 tail code 355, No. 2 *Buntai*, crashed Guadalcanal 10 June 1943 pilot Lieutenant Nonaka Yu'usaburo

This bomber went missing in the late evening of 10 June 1943 during a night nuisance raid over Guadalcanal, when it drove into a cliff in poor visibility at around 2,000 feet altitude behind Henderson Field. Unusually, the bomber had its tail number and markings applied in yellow, confirmed from the wreckage which was discovered in 1993 about fifteen miles west of Henderson Field.

Profile 85 – Mitsubishi G4M1 Model 11 tail code 377 crashed Guadalcanal 30 June 1943, pilot FPO2c Kouno Hachiro

This bomber was among a *chutai* of nine No. 705 *Ku* Bettys which participated with other Betty units in the bombing of US shipping off Rendova on 30 June 1943. Just four bombers returned to Vunakanau while one ditched off New Georgia. This bomber was one of four which went missing. It had in fact crashed along the north Guadalcanal coast, almost 200 miles east of its target. It was likely downed by VMF-122 Corsair pilot Lieutenant Henry Bourgeois after being shot up over target and flying in the wrong direction.

Profile 86 – Mitsubishi G4M1 Model 11, MN1463, tail code 379, *hokoku* HK-1006 第五五全日本號 (55th All Japan)

This bomber was dedicated as a *hokoku* aircraft on 4 November 1942 at the Kyoritsu Auditorium, Tokyo, a building then renown throughout Japan for its modern design. The bomber flew its first mission with No. 705 *Ku* on 6 January 1943 and it appears it survived its tour in the South Seas as it is not listed for the remainder of 1943 as a combat or accidental loss.

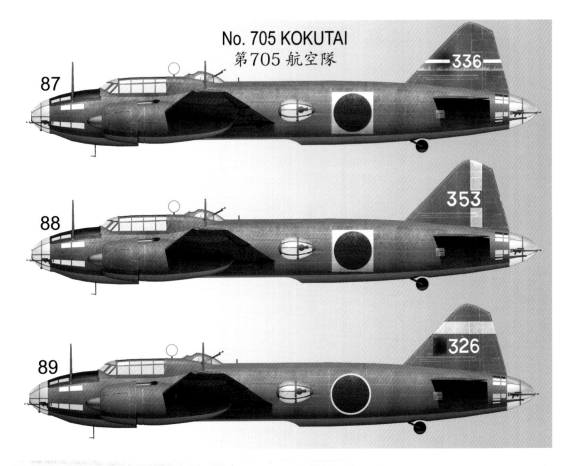

No. 705 KOKUTAI
第705航空隊

87

88

89

336

353

326

No. 705 Ku G4M1 tail code 336, as illustrated in Profile 87, lies abandoned at Munda showcasing its transitional tail markings.

Profile 87 – Mitsubishi G4M1 Model 11, MN 5749, tail code 336

The tail markings on this bomber showcase the transition between the Misawa *Ku* to No. 705 *Ku*. The bomber first served in No. 2 *Buntai* as H-336 then after the transition to No. 705 *Ku* it became "336" in No. 5 *Buntai*. It was abandoned at Munda after it force-landed there on an unknown date around December 1942 after being shot up over Guadalcanal. Note the previous remnants of the wide horizontal band from its days in No. 2 *Buntai* as H-336, over which the new horizontal stripe has been applied.

Profile 88 – Mitsubishi G4M1 Model 11, MN 5569, tail code 353, shot down 14 April 1943 pilot FPO2c Sagara Masao

This bomber was shot down by RAAF Kittyhawks over Milne Bay during Operation *I-Go* on 14 April 1943. A witness to the RAAF attack was Hino Tokichi, a civilian press corps representative aboard an accompanying No. 705 *Ku* Betty, whose pilot dived down to avoid the attack:

> Our bombers avoided the enemy attack through crafty manoeuvres. Then, my body floated in the air, and my head hit the ceiling. Boxes and articles fell from the shelf, and paper scattered everywhere in the terrible rocking movement of the aircraft.

The combined line-abreast fusillade by the Kittyhawks downed two Bettys, one being this bomber. Sagara lost control of "353" which dived into a jungle mountainside near the village of Hioge-Hioge. The day's miracle was fortunate waist gunner Flyer1c Yonekura Shiro who survived the impact. He was subsequently captured by Australian soldiers and became a POW.

Profile 89 – Mitsubishi G4M1 Model 11, tail code 326

This bomber was photographed airborne on 8 December 1942 during a mission to Guadalcanal, shortly after the transition to No. 705 *Ku*. Its tail markings reflect transitionary markings of the former Misawa *Ku* No. 2 *Buntai* with the broad white tail band, with the painted-out prefix "H". It was lost to combat or an accident on an unknown date after 11 January 1943.

G4M1 hokoku HK-860, the subject of Profile 83, undergoes pre-flight preparations at Buin in the early morning.

The Kisarazu Ku transport Betty with tail code R-902, as depicted in Profile 94, lies wrecked and abandoned at Lae.

An early Model 11 Kisarazu Ku Betty with kumogata camouflage and two tail stripes denoting No. 3 Buntai is framed by a Nell at Vunakanau

CHAPTER 20
Kisarazu/No. 707 *Kokutai*

The Kisarazu and Kanoya *Ku* were the oldest bomber units in the IJN, both of which had operated Nells in the China theatre. When the Kisarazu *Ku* was re-equipped with the modern G4M1 Betty it was initially established as a land-attack training unit operating from Kisarazu Air Base on the southern shore of Tokyo Bay. It was reorganised into a combat unit during the IJN restructure of 1 April 1942, and assigned the tail code prefix "R" to represent the second *Romanji* syllable in the name Kisarazu, as "K" had already been allocated to the Kanoya *Ku*. The restructured *kokutai* was assigned to the 26th Air Flotilla under commanding officer Captain Konishi Yasuo.

The original inventory assignment was three full *chutai* of 27 bombers plus three spares. An advance detachment of five Bettys arrived at Kavieng from Truk on 21 August 1942, from where it conducted a two-hour familiarisation flight the next day, thus constituting the unit's first South Seas mission. The first mission from Vunakanau, Rabaul, took place two days later with a full *chutai* of nine bombers raiding Guadalcanal. The following day fifteen Bettys returned to the same target led by *hikotaicho* Lieutenant Nabeta Miyoshi. By the end of the month the full *kokutai* of three *chutai* had arrived in the South Seas with a small detachment *in situ* at Kavieng to conduct patrols.

Thrown immediately into the Guadalcanal campaign, the unit's losses were straightaway grievous. It lost six bombers to combat in its first month of operations, and ten more throughout September and October. During the late 1942 IJN restructure it was rebadged as No. 707 *Ku* on 1 November after which on 11 and 12 November it lost six more Bettys to combat. This meant that by mid-November its total losses to combat were 22 Bettys, with two more claimed by accidents. With its inventory reduced to a handful, it was decided to disband the unit as a fighting force. Accordingly on 1 December 1942, No. 707 *Ku*'s six remaining crews and Bettys were incorporated into No. 705 *Ku*, and No. 707 *Ku* was officially decommissioned.

Markings

The entire initial Kisarazu *Ku* Betty inventory consisted of early Model 11s in the brown and green *kumogata* camouflage scheme with a white fuselage band denoting assignment to the 26th Air Flotilla. The three *chutai* adopted the following tail codes and markings:

   No. 1 *Buntai/Chutai*, R-301 to R-320 (no tail markings)

   No. 2 *Buntai/Chutai*, R-321 to R-340 (one medium-width white horizontal tail stripe)

   No. 3 *Buntai/Chutai*, R-341 to R-360 (two medium-width narrow horizontal tail stripes)

The No. 705 *Ku* mission log shows that five of the six surviving Bettys amalgamated from No. 707 *Ku* on 1 December 1942 were R-302, R-305, R-308, R-333 and R-338. These aircraft were later renumbered by No. 705 *Ku*, but it is possible some retained their original numbers.

KISARAZU/ No. 707 KOKUTAI
木更津／第707航空隊

90 R-310

91 R-333

92 R-351

93 R-360

94 R-902

Profile 90 – G4M1 Model 11, tail code R-310, No. 1 *Buntai*

This bomber was photographed heading to Guadalcanal in October 1942. It was one of the original Kisarazu *Ku* Bettys which arrived at Rabaul in August 1942.

Profile 91 – G4M1 Model 11, tail code R-333, No. 2 *Buntai*

This bomber was one of the original Kisarazu *Ku* bombers which arrived at Rabaul in August 1942, and was one of the six surviving Bettys transferred to No. 705 *Ku* on 1 December 1942. The single horizontal tail stripe denotes No. 2 *Buntai*.

Profile 92 – G4M1 Model 11 tail code R-351, No. 3 *Buntai*, shot down 12 September 1942, pilot Lieutenant (jg) Takamatsu Naoichi

This Betty flown by Lieutenant (jg) Takamatsu Naoichi, crashed into heavy jungle on the perimeter of Henderson Field on 12 September 1942 after it was shot down by Wildcats. The airframe was subsequently heavily souvenired by US soldiers shortly afterwards. The bomber was a replacement new Model 11 in overall green.

Profile 93 – G4M1 Model 11, tail code R-360, No. 3 *Buntai*

This G4M1 was photographed returning to Rabaul after a strike on Guadalcanal in late 1942. The bomber was another replacement new Model 11 in overall green, with the two horizontal tail stripes denoting service with No. 3 *Buntai/Chutai*.

Profile 94 – G4M1 Model 11 MN 419, tail code R-902, 11th Air Fleet

This bomber was the second transport Betty assigned to serve with the Kisarazu *Ku*, although it fell under the administrative command of the 11th Air Fleet. Accordingly, it lacks the white fuselage band denoting assignment to the 26th Air Flotilla.

G4M1 tail code R-360, as illustrated in Profile 93, airborne during a Guadalcanal mission.

An early silver Toko Ku Mavis, tail code O-13, flying a patrol.

Toko Ku Mavis O-46, as depicted in Profile 95, moored in the Shortlands in mid-1942.

CHAPTER 21
Toko/No. 851 *Kokutai*

The Toko *Ku* was a reconnaissance flying boat unit formed on 1 October 1940 at the port of Toko, Taiwan (*Toko* translates as "frozen harbour"). Initially equipped with two dozen H6K Mavis flying boats, it was assigned to the 21ˢᵗ Air Flotilla and later from June 1942 it also operated two H8K1 Emily Flying Boats. The unit also trialled the A6M2-N Rufe floatplane fighter, however this detachment never served in the South Seas, and was instead sent to the Kurile Islands to the northeast of Japan.

Meanwhile, the main Mavis unit was sent to Palau at the start of the Pacific War, but throughout 1942 detachments roamed far and wide, from Rabaul to the Netherlands East Indies. From late August 1942, three flying boat units, No. 14, Yokohama and Toko *Ku*, combined in the South Seas to effectively operate as a team. It became commonplace for crews to borrow flying boats from other units, and the same missions are sometimes duplicated in operational logs of multiple units.

Toko *Ku* Mavises set up bases in the Shortland Islands and Rabaul in early September 1942 to supplement Yokohama *Ku* flying boats which had incurred substantial losses during the first month of the Guadalcanal campaign. Then on 12 September 1942 the remnants of the decimated Yokohama *Ku*, three Mavis flying boats and crews, were amalgamated into the Toko *Ku*. On 1 November 1942, the Toko *Ku* was rebadged as No. 851 *Ku*. By then its headquarters had moved from Rabaul to the Shortland Islands.

The unit's *hikotaicho* was Lieutenant Commander Wada Shigemi who was replaced by Lieutenant Commander Ikegami Tsutomu on 15 December 1942. No. 851 *Ku* flew its last mission in the South Seas from the Shortland Islands on 25 February 1943 after which Ikegami oversighted the unit's transfer to Surabaya in the Netherlands East Indies. Its flying boats nonetheless continued to visit Rabaul for liaison purposes until early 1944.

Arguably No. 851 *Ku*'s landmark mission commenced in the late afternoon of 20 January 1943 when one of its H8K1 Emilys departed the Shortlands and arrived overhead Espiritu Santo in the New Hebrides at exactly midnight. There it loitered overhead for 45 minutes such that the Americans below thought several aircraft were involved. At 0045 hours the Emily logged:

> Reconnaissance and bombing mission completed. Destroyed the military base and left four fires burning.

In fact, the few 60-kilogram bombs dropped did little damage, impacting around the USN repair and oil storage facility at Aore Island where a plantation cow was killed. Nonetheless the nearby harbour that night was indeed full of warships including four cruisers and four destroyers. The unforeseen raid raised eyebrows in Washington, as Secretary of the Navy Frank Knox was overnighting at the location on an inspection tour at the time.

Markings

The initial Mavis inventory appeared in NMF over which silver lacquer was applied, some of which appeared early in the South Seas theatre on liaison missions. Codes were also painted in black on the wing undersurfaces. All later flying boats were painted in green and bore a white fuselage band denoting association with the 21st Air Flotilla. The Toko *Ku* was allocated the tail prefix "O", which was changed to "N2" in fleet orders after the unit became No. 851 *Ku*. However, the "N2" prefix was not implemented, and it was changed to "851" instead. All codes on green camouflaged hulls were applied in white.

An early silver Toko Ku Mavis with the code O-32 painted on the wing undersurface.

A No. 851 Ku Mavis moored at Rabaul in November 1943. The tail code is 851-02.

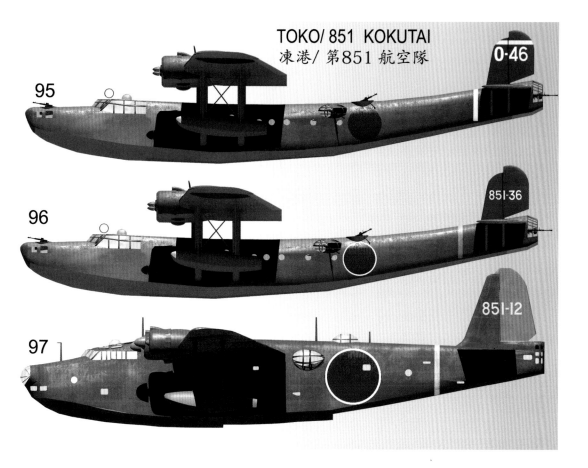

TOKO/ 851 KOKUTAI
凍港/ 第851 航空隊

95

96

97

Profile 95 – Kawanishi H6K4 Mavis tail code O-46

This Toko *Ku* Mavis was photographed anchored in the Shortlands in mid-1942.

Profile 96 – Kawanishi H6K4 Mavis tail code 851-36

On 21 November 1942, while under the command of Lieutenant Tsuneo Hitsuji, this No. 851 *Ku* Mavis was flying a patrol south of Guadalcanal when it encountered an 11th BG B-17E Flying Fortress. An ensuring gun fight saw both aircraft damaged. When the Mavis taxied back inside Shortland harbour saltwater flooded the hull as the airframe had sustained ninety-three bullet holes.

Profile 97 – Kawanishi H8K2 Emily tail code 851-14

This No. 851 *Ku* Emily flying boat operated into Rabaul during liaison visits in late 1943.

The single stripe on these two No. 702 Ku Bettys at Vunakanau in late 1943 show second generation markings of No. 1 Chutai.

CHAPTER 22
No. 702 *Kokutai*

This unit was established during the IJN November restructure following the rebuilding of No. 4 *Ku* in Japan after its decimation during the Guadalcanal campaign. After it was reassigned to the 25th Air Flotilla, the unit ferried itself back to the South Seas theatre. On 28 April 1943 the first detachment of two Bettys left Kisarazu, each carrying ten ground crew as passengers, staging to Vunakanau via Tinian, Truk and Kavieng. The remainder of the inventory arrived on 14 May 1943 with 37 new G4M1 Model 11s. Similar to its predecessor No. 4 *Ku*, No. 702 *Ku* incurred substantive losses in the South Seas and was decommissioned on 1 December 1943.

Commanding officer Captain Kuno Shuji led the unit for its return to Rabaul until deactivation. In an intriguing salute to the complications of the Japanese language, the unit was colloquially referred to among the unit's cadre as either the "Hisano Unit" or the "Kuno Unit". The reason was a play on the *kanji* for Kuno's surname (久野) which can be pronounced either way.

No. 702 *Ku*'s first combat loss was a solitary Betty sent over Port Moresby for a night nuisance raid on 15 May 1943. For two weeks in mid-May 1943 a detachment of Bettys from Nos. 1 and 6 *Buntai* was deployed to Ballale Island to fly armed reconnaissance missions over the Solomon Islands. On 23 May 1943 six Bettys from Ballale damaged the torpedo boat tender USS *Niagara* southeast of San Cristobal. Although further detachments were based at Ballale throughout June, during the evening of 29/30 June 1943 the island was bombarded heavily by gunfire from a USN task force. Afterwards, the detachment withdrew to Vunakanau after abandoning five airframes which had been damaged during the bombardment. Small numbers of the unit's bombers nonetheless returned to Ballale over the forthcoming months to conduct more patrols.

On the afternoon of 30 June 1943, the No. 702 *Ku* Bettys participated in the second Japanese bombing raid against the USN invasion force off Rendova. The formation comprised 26 G4M1 torpedo-armed Bettys (seventeen from No. 702 *Ku* with nine more from No. 705 *Ku*). The Betty formation and fighter escort were intercepted by US Wildcats and Corsairs and were also targeted by ship-based anti-aircraft guns. In total nineteen Bettys and seventeen crews were lost including G4M1 Betty tail code U2-343 which crashed on Rendova. Only three No. 702 *Ku* Bettys returned safely and a fourth ditched with the crew rescued.

On 4 September the unit lost six Bettys against the Red Beach landing just east of Lae, and two more to P-70 night fighters over Guadalcanal on 21 September. It then lost nine more during night attacks from 1 to 19 November during Operation *Ro-Go*. In the space of only five months the unit suffered the catastrophic loss of 52 bombers to combat or accidents. On 1 December the remaining handful of aircraft and crews was transferred to No. 751 *Ku* and the unit was decommissioned.

Markings

No end of confusion has been published about over the markings of No. 702 *Ku*, largely because the unit underwent two separate markings regimes. This is complicated by a hybrid markings regime resulting from a crossover encompassing both administrative and operational structures. When it left Japan No. 702 *Ku* was structured thus:

No. 1 *Buntai* (administrative), Lieutenant Takahama Haruo, *chutaicho* of No. 3 *Chutai*

No. 2 *Buntai* (administrative), Lieutenant (jg) Matsumaru Saburo, *chutaicho* of No. 4 *Chutai*

No. 5 *Buntai* (administrative), Lieutenant (jg) Yagita Nagayoshi, *chutaicho* of No. 1 *Chutai*

No. 6 *Buntai* (administrative), Lieutenant (jg) Furu'uchi Osamu, *chutaicho* of No. 2 *Chutai*

When the Bettys left Japan, they carried the new tail code prefix "U2" which had been allocated to No. 702 *Ku* by the 25th Air Flotilla. Aircraft numbers were issued sequentially according to the administrative *buntai*, however tail markings indicated the operational *chutai*. Furthermore, most *buntai* commanders ordered the tail prefix "U2" painted over for security reasons shortly after arrival in Rabaul, but not all. Exceptions included No. 2 *Buntai* (No. 4 *Chutai*) which retained the prefix. When the bombers first arrived at Rabaul the Bettys were officially marked thus, bearing in mind most prefixes were painted out:

No. 1 *Buntai* tail codes U2-301 to U2-320, three stripes (unit marking for No. 3 *Chutai*)

No. 2 *Buntai* tail codes U2-321 to U2-340, one broad narrow stripe above, then one narrow stripe (unit marking for No. 4 *Chutai*)

No. 5 *Buntai* tail codes U2-341 to U2-360, one stripe (unit marking for No. 1 *Chutai*)

No. 6 *Buntai* tail codes U2-361 to U2-380, two stripes (unit marking for No. 2 *Chutai*)

To further complicate matters a revised markings regime was instituted around mid-June 1943 in order to realign the numerical sequence with the renumbered *chutai*. Tail prefixes were painted over, leaving this modified structure:

No.1 *Daitai*

No.1 *Chutai* tail codes 301 to 320 one stripe across fin

No.2 *Chutai* tail codes 321 to 340 two stripes across fin

No. 2 *Daitai*

No.3 *Chutai* tail codes 341 to 360 one rudder stripe

No.4 *Chutai* tail codes 361 to 380 one thin rudder stripe on top of one thick one

The wreck of tail code U2-343 (see Profile 99) as it came to rest on Rendova Island.

No. 702 Ku Betty 356 at Vunakanau in late 1943 carries one rudder stripe showcasing No. 3 Chutai's second generation markings. The numerals are placed to the right indicating this airframe originally had the prefix "U2" applied, but which has since been painted out.

No. 702 KOKUTAI
第702航空隊

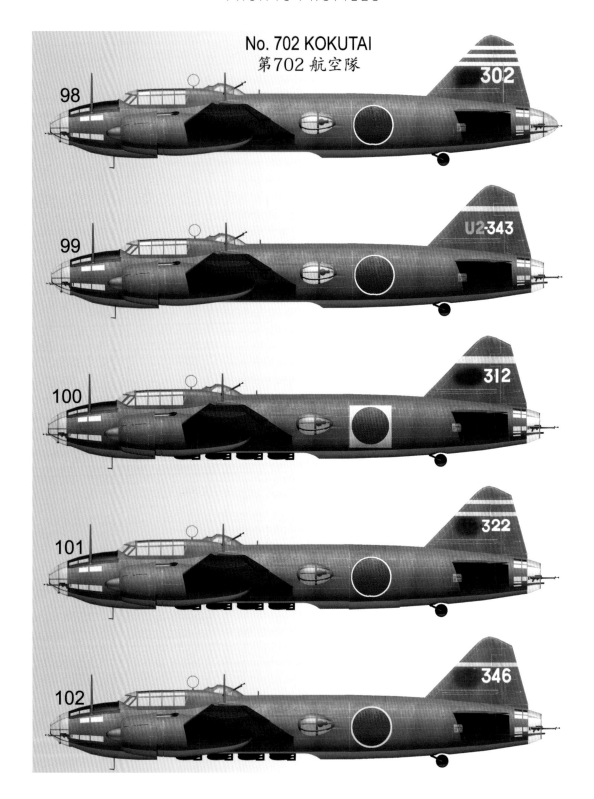

98

99

100

101

102

302

U2-343

312

322

346

Profile 98 – G4M1 Model 11 tail code 302, ditched 17 June 1943, FCPO Yokogawa Shigeo

This bomber was damaged by anti-aircraft fire over Port Moresby on the night of 16 June 1943, and ditched off New Guinea's northern coast in the early hours of the following morning. After FCPO Yokogawa Shigeo ditched the bomber he and two others were captured and made POW when they made landfall a few days later. The crew confirmed the bomber had three stripes on the fin during interrogation, reflecting assignment to No. 1 *Buntai* (administrative), but operationally it was assigned to No. 3 *Chutai*.

Profile 99 – G4M1 tail code U2-343 shot down 30 June 1943, Rendova Island

This bomber crashed on Rendova Island on the afternoon of 30 June 1943 following the second Japanese bombing raid against the nearby USN invasion force. The No. 702 *Ku* formation comprised seventeen Bettys alongside nine more from No. 705 *Ku*. This G4M1 with an unidentified crew was one shot down by either fighters or ship-based anti-aircraft fire. The bomber carries one fin stripe of the No. 1 *Chutai* first generation markings, and photos from the crash site show a yellow "U2" prefix.

Profile 100 – G4M1 Model 11 tail code 312, shot down 30 June 1943

This G4M1 is another which crashed on the afternoon of 30 June 1943 in the second Japanese Rendova bombing raid. The unidentified crew was also lost to either US fighters or ship-based anti-aircraft fire. The bomber carries one fin stripe of the No. 1 *Chutai* first generation markings, however the yellow "U2" prefix was painted out.

Profile 101 – G4M1 Model 11 tail code 322

This bomber was photographed at Vunakanau in July 1943 with two fin stripes of the No. 2 *Chutai* first generation markings and with the yellow "U2" prefix painted out.

Profile 102 – G4M1 Model 11 MN 2671, tail code 346, shot up 17 July 1943, pilot FCPO Matsuoka Shigenobu

On 17 July 1943 FCPO Matsuoka Shigenobu landed this Betty at Ballale at 0230 after it was damaged over Guadalcanal by night fighters. The bomber had five deceased crew aboard, however following field repairs Matsuoka returned to Vunakanau with a scratch crew late that afternoon. The bomber carries one tail stripe of the No. 1 *Chutai* first generation markings and has the "U2" prefix painted out.

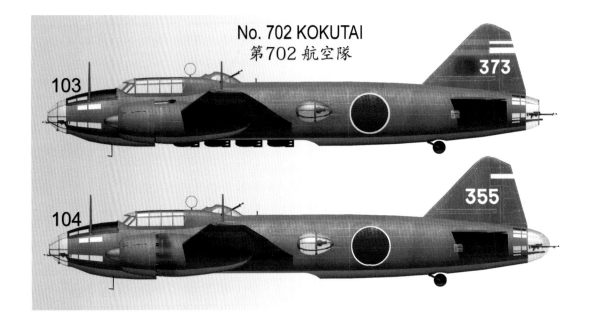

Profile 103 – G4M1 tail code 373, shot down 30 June 1943, pilot FPO2c Hironaga Atsushi

FPO2c Hironaga Atsushi and his crew of seven were lost on the afternoon of 30 June 1943 in the second Japanese bombing raid against Rendova, either intercepted by US fighters or hit by ship-based anti-aircraft fire. The bomber carries one broad and one thin rudder stripe representing No. 4 *Chutai*'s second generation markings and has the "U2" prefix painted out. Note also the barely-visible legacy two stripe marking from first generation markings.

Profile 104 – G4M1 tail code 355, crashed off Bougainville 17 November 1943, No. 3 *Chutai*, observer Warrant Officer Yamabe Toshio

This bomber crashed into the water off Bougainville at around 0300 on the morning of 17 November 1943 after sustaining return fire from USN ships it had attacked. Tail gunner Flyer1c Honda Yoshiro, the sole survivor, was made POW by a passing USN destroyer. This Betty is a replacement late Model 11 with a "clam-shell" rear gun housing and individual exhaust stacks. The bomber carries one rudder stripe showcasing second generation No. 3 *Chutai* markings with the numeral 355 centrally applied on the fin.

Bomber 370 at Vunakanau in late 1943 showing one broad and one thin rudder stripe representing No. 4 Chutai second generation markings with the "U2" prefix removed.

Photographed at Vunakanau during a low-level strike of 24 October 1943, this Betty retains the first-generation twin fin stripes of No. 2 Chutai, with the "U2" prefix removed.

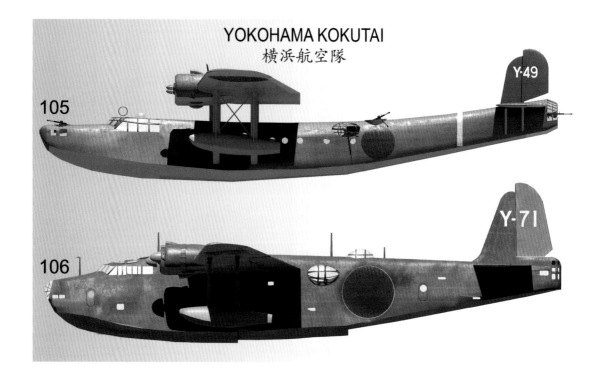

YOKOHAMA KOKUTAI
横浜航空隊

Profile 105 – Kawanishi H6K2 Mavis, tail code Y-49

This early model Mavis was sunk at its moorings on 7 August 1942 during the first USN attack against Gavutu, near Tulagi. Maintenance documents were later salvaged from the wreckage by US intelligence.

Profile 106 – H8K1 Emily tail code Y-71, aircraft commander Captain Hashizume Toshio

H8K1 Emilys tail codes Y-71 and Y-72 were both pre-production aircraft built by Kawanishi in 1941, both of which bombed Pearl Harbor on 6 March 1942, after which they proceeded to Malaguna anchorage, Rabaul. On morning of 10 March 1942 both departed to patrol Sectors A and F on a routine search for enemy ships. Y-72 returned to Rabaul at 1540 that afternoon, however Y-71 commanded by Captain Hashizume Toshio failed to return.

Yokohama Ku Mavis tail code Y-41 seen moored in the Shortlands.

CHAPTER 23
Yokohama *Kokutai*

From the Pacific War's commencement, the core of the IJN South Seas air reconnaissance capability was the flying boats of the Yokohama *Ku*. Formed in Yokohama on 1 October 1936 as a naval patrol unit, and initially equipped with six Hiro H4H flying boats, on 1 December 1941 it was re-equipped with 24 H6K4 Mavis flying boats and assigned to support Fourth Fleet operations. In this month it flew three bombing raids against Rabaul, as well as missions to Wake Island.

Following the invasion of Rabaul on 23 January 1942, four days later a dozen Mavises deployed to Rabaul, staging via the advance island base at Kapingamarangi from Truk. On 28 January a solitary Mavis reconnoitred Port Moresby, marking the first time a Japanese aircraft flew over the town. By the beginning of February 1942, Lieutenant Commander Tashiro Soichi's had set up the Yokohama *Ku* headquarters at Rabaul, anchoring most of their Mavises near Lakunai airfield from where they could use IJN facilities being built there.

On the first day of February 1942, the *kokutai* undertook arguably its most unusual mission when nine Mavises cruised into New Guinea's mountains behind Lae and bombed the small town of Wau. The month also saw the Yokohama *Ku* furnished with two H8K1 Emily flying boats, a pre-production model of the series.

On 14 July 1942 the Yokohama *Ku* was reassigned to the 25th Air Flotilla. Following the 7 August 1942 US Marine invasion of Guadalcanal, the unit was reduced to six Mavises when the entire Tulagi detachment, with one exception which had left early that morning, was sunk at its moorings. The remaining flying boats continued long-range reconnaissance missions from Rabaul and the Shortlands, serving as the eyes of the 11th Air Fleet until mid-September 1942. The unit nonetheless continued to suffer heavy losses. The early stages of the Solomons campaign in particular proved costly, to the extent that by mid-September 1942 the Yokohama *Ku* had ceased to exist as an effective fighting force. Its surviving personnel were sent back to Japan and on 12 September 1942 the few remaining flying boats were redistributed to the Toko *Ku*.

The Yokohama *Ku* was redesignated as No. 801 *Ku* on 1 November 1942, however by then it had returned to Japan, and the unit never returned to the South Seas.

Markings

When the Yokohama *Ku* first arrived at Rabaul the Mavis inventory appeared in NMF with a protective seaworthy lacquer. These were gradually replaced by green Mavises, and when reassigned to the 25th Air Flotilla from the Fourth Fleet on 14 July 1942, these all received a white fuselage band to indicate flotilla association. The tail code prefix remained "Y" throughout the unit's time in the theatre.

Outside the scope of this volume, the unit also deployed a contingent of the early production Nakajima A6N2-N Rufe fighter seaplanes the first of which arrived at Tulagi in the Solomons on 3 June 1942 (see *Pacific Profiles Volume Eight*).

No. 751 Ku G4M1 Z2-313, as depicted in Profile 111, just before it was shot down north of New Guinea in early 1944.

Kanoya Ku Betty K-324 in the foreground with K-327 behind it (see Profile 108). These have been photographed during the Guadalcanal campaign, with the curvy camouflage demarcation on display.

CHAPTER 24
Kanoya/No. 751 *Kokutai*

The penultimate chapter is reserved for the Kanoya *Ku* which, alongside its sister unit the Kisarazu *Ku*, was one of the first two land bomber units established by the IJN. Both operated Nells in the China theatre. The Kanoya *Ku*, which later became No. 751 *Ku* in the late 1942 restructure, served the longest of any IJN combat unit in the South Seas.

The Kanoya *Ku* was re-equipped with the modern G4M1 Betty in November 1940 and allocated the tail code prefix "K" when assigned to the 21st Air Flotilla. Although initially established solely as a land-attack bomber unit, during the 1 April 1942 IJN restructure a Zero fighter wing was attached to the unit (see *Pacific Profiles Volume Five*). The Zero wing was created as the Kanoya *Ku*'s No. 3 *Chutai* at Don Muang airfield, north of Bangkok. Then on 1 October 1942 as part of the IJN restructure, the fighter wing was made an independent unit and redesignated No. 253 *Ku*. On 1 September 1943 No. 751 *Ku* unit was reassigned to the 25th Air Flotilla.

Due to his theatre experience, the former Misawa *Ku hikotaicho* Lieutenant Commander Nakamura Tomo'o led the unit's first combat mission of nine Bettys to Guadalcanal on 13 September 1942. On 16 September 1942, *chutaicho* Lieutenant Nabeta Miyoshi took another *chutai* of eight Bettys to Rabaul as an advanced echelon. On 1 December 1943 the remaining three No. 702 *Ku* Bettys, a unit which had fought itself to a standstill (see Chapter 22), were transferred to No. 751 *Ku*. The *kokutai* was the only one to briefly operate the G4M2 from Rabaul, a completely different airframe to the G4M1.

During its time in the South Seas No. 751 *Ku* continued to maintain detachments at Kavieng and outside the theatre at Sabang in the Netherlands East Indies. Its last ten bombers were evacuated from Rabaul to Truk in early February 1944 whilst its ground crew were evacuated from Rabaul aboard the transport ships *Kowa Maru* and *Kokai Maru* on 20 February 1944. The *Kowa Maru* was sunk a few days later by USAAF bombers, and the capture of dozens of No. 751 *Ku* personnel by USN destroyers resulted in a trove of intelligence. The unit was administratively decommissioned on 10 July 1944, however had it had ceased to operate as a fighting force some months prior.

The unit lost just two Bettys to combat as the Kanoya *Ku*, but the staggering amount of 102 bombers as No. 751 *Ku*. The very last combat loss from Rabaul took place on 17 February 1944.

Markings

Following the 1 April 1942 IJN restructure, the Kanoya *Ku*'s bomber wing was allocated an official strength of 54 Bettys which were divided into six *buntai/chutai* split between two *daitai*, reflecting its China theatre structure:

No. 1 *Daitai*

No. 1 *Chutai*, tail codes K-301 to K-315 (no markings)

No. 2 *Chutai*, tail codes K-316 to K-330 (one white stripe)

No. 3 *Chutai*, tail codes K-331 to K-345 (two white stripes)

<u>No. 2 *Daitai*</u>

No. 4 *Chutai*, tail codes K-351 to K-365 (one thin white stripe at top)

No. 5 *Chutai*, tail codes K-366 to K-380 (two widely spaced white stripes)

No. 6 *Chutai*, tail codes K-381 to K-399 (three white stripes, two narrow ones on bottom)

A single white fuselage band indicated the Kanoya *Ku*'s assignment to the 21st Air Flotilla, and the initial inventory of Bettys all bore brown and green camouflage. On 1 October 1942 the unit was rebadged as No. 751 *Ku* and all "K" prefixes were painted out. In June 1943 the *kokutai* was issued the new tail code prefix "Z2", however in the South Seas in many cases this was painted over, or not applied on security grounds. Several Bettys operating from Truk during this time and operating into Rabaul nonetheless carried the code.

When the unit was reassigned to the 25th Air Flotilla on 1 September 1943, its markings were changed again, this time without any *chutai* markings, and the previous fuselage band was painted out. A new tail prefix "51" was applied from early December 1943 onwards, and the *kokutai* was divided into four *chutai*. However captured documents indicated the official allocations were never met, with the actual inventory structured thus:

No. 1 *Chutai*, allocated codes 51-301 to 51-320 (actual 301-303, 305-307, 308-310 spare 311)

No. 2 *Chutai*, allocated codes 51-321 to 51-340 (actual 321-323, 325-327, 328-330 spare 331)

No. 5 *Chutai*, allocated codes 51-341 to 51-360 (actual 341-343, 345-347, 348-350 spare 351)

No. 6 *Chutai*, allocated codes 51-361 to 51-380 (actual 361-363, 365-367, 368-370 spare 371)

No. 751 Ku Betty tail code 51-352 shows the new prefix "51" applied after 1 September 1943 when the unit was reassigned to the 25th Air Flotilla.

KANOYA/ No. 751 KOKUTAI
鹿屋/ 第751 航空隊

K-357
107

K-327
108

378
109

Profile 107 – G4M1 Model 11, tail code K-357, No. 4 *Chutai*

This Kanoya *Ku* bomber was among the initial inventory painted in the brown and green camouflage scheme. The single white fuselage band indicates assignment to the 21st Air Flotilla. This bomber was photographed as a participant in the Guadalcanal campaign.

Profile 108 – G4M1 Model 11, tail code K-327, No. 2 *Chutai*

Also photographed during the Guadalcanal campaign, K-327 displays the curved camouflage demarcation line which featured on the first batches of overall green Model 11s to leave Mitsubishi's factory.

Profile 109 – G4M1 Model 11, tail code 378, No. 5 *Chutai*, shot down 12 April 1943, FCPO Nagamatsu Hiroshi

On 12 April 1943 during Operation *I-Go*, multiple Lightning and Airacobra attacks fragmented incoming Betty formations attacking Port Moresby. Lightning pilot Lieutenant Richard Smith chased this No. 751 *Ku* Betty all the way to Mount Albert Edward. FCPO Nagamatsu Hiroshi maintained limited control, but with reduced power from a shot-out engine, he finally crashed into the side of the mountain at 9,500 feet where the impact broke the bomber's back.

KANOYA/ No. 751 KOKUTAI
鹿屋/第751航空隊

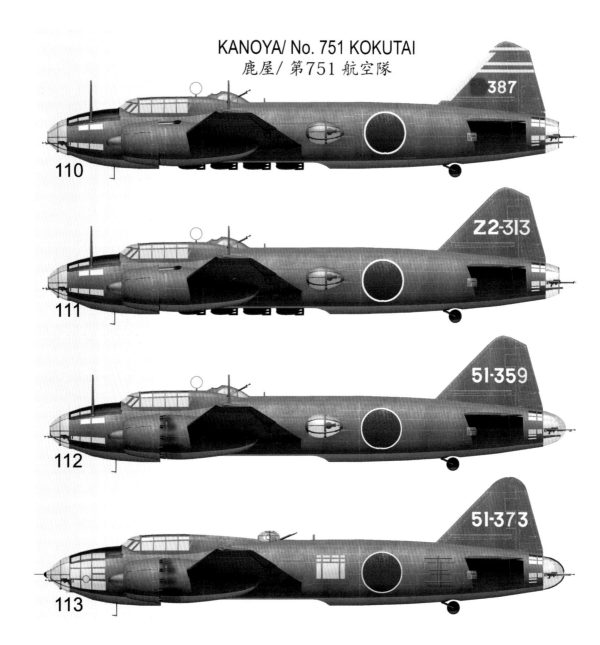

110

111

112

113

Profile 110 – G4M1 Model 11, tail code 387, No. 6 *Chutai*

No. 751 *Ku* G4M1 387 displays white piping on its *hinomaru* indicating it was among late 1943 batches of overall green Model 11s to leave Mitsubishi's factory. Note the pattern of two lower stripes and one upper one.

Profile 111 – G4M1 Model 11, tail code Z2-313, No. 1 *Chutai*

When the Kanoya *Ku* was rebadged as No. 751 *Ku* it was allocated a new tail code prefix "Z2", however in the South Seas in most cases this was painted over, or not applied on security grounds. Several Bettys operating from Truk at the time nonetheless carried the code, but it is unclear how many also did so in Rabaul, if any. This bomber was shot down during combat with Allied aircraft north of New Guinea in early 1944.

Profile 112 – G4M1 Model 11 MN 6119, tail code 51-359, pilot FPO1c Tsuzuku Toshiakai

On 24 January 1944 FPO1c Tsuzuku Toshiakai force-landed near Kavieng. The bomber was one of five which departed Vunakanau at dawn that morning to conduct sector patrols, however the region was plagued by bad weather. One Betty made its way to Kavieng as a safe haven an hour and a half after departing Vunakanau, whilst the other four landed there around lunchtime in order to refuel before attempting to return home to Vunakanau. Tsuzuku as the most experienced and senior pilot, set out around 1400 to see if the route home was negotiable, however he soon became cut-off by weather. Around half an hour later he force-landed, coming down gear up into a *kunai* grass plain about ten miles south of Kavieng airfield. At the time of publication, the remains of the bomber were still *in situ*. This Betty is a late Model 11 with the redesigned rear "clamshell" gondola for the tail gunner.

Profile 113 – G4M2 Model 22-*ko* tail code 51-373

This radar-equipped Model 22 was among four new aircraft flown to Vunakanau in early February 1944, and the diary of a ground-crew member shows 51-373 as the last to arrive. The bomber was one of four sent down from Truk for ongoing trials from Rabaul for night operations, equipped with an H6 radar as indicated by the antennae on the rear fuselage. Note that this is a substantially different airframe to the G4M1, with rear "clamshell" gondola, water-injection engines, square side gun positions, a different design glasshouse nose, circular dorsal turret and rounded fin.

K-308 and K-312 from the Kanoya Ku's No. 1 Chutai are discernible in this photograph taken early in the Guadalcanal campaign.

OKAMOTO BUNTAI
岡 本 分 隊

114

115

116

Profile 114 – A5M4 Chitose *Ku* tail code S-123, No. 4 *Ku* tail code F-123

This Claude was photographed at Rabaul in early January 1942 as S-123 with a pre-war red tail. It became F-123 following the conversion to No. 4 *Ku*.

Profile 115 – A5M4 Chitose *Ku* tail code S-153, 報國 – 373 (伊勢丹號) *Hokoku* - 373 Donated by the Isetan Company

Known tail codes of Chitose *Ku* A5M4s being unpacked at Roi in late 1941 include S-118, S-153, S-158 and S-160. The rear fuselages of S-153 and S-160 both had *hokoku* inscriptions.

Profile 116 – A5M4 No. 4 *Ku* tail code F-103

F-103 was a *shotaicho* fighter assigned to the Okamoto *Buntai* at Rabaul in early February 1942.

CHAPTER 25

Okamoto *Buntai*
(Chitose/No. 4/Tainan *Kokutai* Fighter Detachment)

The deployment of the A5M4 Claude falls outside *Pacific Profiles Volume Five* (land based Zero fighter units), so is covered in this volume. The Chitose *Ku* operated the first land-based fighters in the South Seas. A detachment of A5M4 Claude fighters operated from Rabaul, Gasmata and Lae from late January until early April 1942. The detachment operated under three distinct unit banners. However, throughout it retained its colloquial name the "Okamoto *Buntai*" named after its unit commander, Lieutenant Okamoto Harutoshi.

Okamoto led a detachment of Chitose *Ku* Claudes which were ferried from Truk to the newly captured Rabaul via aircraft carriers where they arrived on 31 January 1942. No. 4 *Ku* was established on 10 February 1942 and with one stroke of the pen the Okamoto *chutai* of the Chitose *Ku* became its fighter wing. Later on 1 April the detachment was assimilated into the Tainan *Ku*. In its brief life the detachment operated a total of fifteen A5M4s Claudes in the South Seas.

Markings

The A5M4s initially retained their Chitose *Ku* tail codes, using the prefix "S". This was replaced by "F'" when No. 4 *Ku* was formed. It is doubtful the Tainan *Ku* "V" prefix was ever applied to any Claudes. Clear photographs do exist of Claudes with a 'V" prefix however these date from the pre-war era showing a training unit operating from a carrier.

Chitose *Ku* markings used one band to denote *shotaicho* status, and two bands for a *chutaicho*, with their colour denoting the *chutai* to which they were assigned. The Okamoto *chutai* sported black, and was allocated six A5M4s and ten Zeros, tail codes F-101 through to F-116. It appears the Iwasaki *chutai* (Lieutenant Iwasaki Nobuhiro) used red as a unit colour, although this is yet to be confirmed. It had an allocated strength of six A5M4s and eleven Zeros with tail codes F-120 through to F-136. The Kawai *chutai* (Lieutenant Kawai Shiro) applied yellow bands and operated three A5M4s and eleven Zeros coded F-140 through to F-153.

After 1 April 1942 the Tainan *Ku* adopted and expanded No. 4 *Ku*'s *chutai* structure, although with increasing numbers of A6M2s available the A5M4s were retired. Just ten Claudes remained at Rabaul, and these were loaded aboard the *Montevideo Maru* on 21 June 1942. The airframes never reached Japan, however, as the ship was sunk during the return voyage off the Philippines.

SOURCES

The language barrier is as formidable today as it was back in WWII, or so it seems. Matters are not assisted by the fact that much IJN legacy *kanji* cannot be read by modern Japanese. Thus many English language books pertaining to IJN matters hold serious inaccuracies as they usually have failed to consult primary Japanese sources. This book only cites primary Japanese sources, however, even so, some are incomplete. By way of example, the Historical Monograph Series - Summary of Aerial Operations in New Guinea & the Solomons (Southeast Naval Operations Parts 1 through 5) was compiled several years after the cessation of hostilities and should only be used as a guide of where else to look. Japanese names in *kanji* can be byzantine, however all herein are sourced from operational logs and can thus be relied upon to be the actual name. Likewise *kokutai* names and numbers are cited from the *Kanji/Romanji* from relevant logs. Listed below are only the main sources, as space precludes listing peripheral ones.

Reports/memoirs of pilots (various units)

Muraoka Shinichi, Tanaguchi Masayoshi, Yoshida Masa'aki, Shimizu Kazuo, Katsuaki Kira, Kimura Toshio, Hasegawa Tomoari. Interrogation reports of Betty crew and ground crew; total of 112 reports translated into English held at the Australian War Memorial, comprising more than 500 pages of intelligence. Specialist interrogations proved particularly useful, e..g Misawa *Ku* engineer FPO2c Yashiki Muneo from Betty H-352 and No. 705 *Ku* Betty crewmembers Matsuo Yasuo, Sakagawa Bun and Yonekura Shiro (the author is acutely aware that many POWs provided false information).

Memoirs/Diaries

Memoirs of Lt-Commander Okumiya Masatake, staff officer to Rear Admiral Kakuta Kakuji

Diary of Rear Admiral Sanwa Yoshiwa, Chief of Staff (aviation), Southeast Area Fleet

Diary of Vice Admiral Kusaka Jinichi, Commander SE Area Fleet, hand-written (1942/ 43)

Manual of Military Secret Orders, ATIS captured document dated 20 July 1943

Japanese Air Terms in *Kanji*, Squadron Leader A. R Boyce, Far Eastern Bureau, Calcutta 1944

Messages, Japanese Naval Forces, September 1942- February 1944 (Allied intercepts)

Japan Times and Advertiser, articles 1942/ 44

Asahi Shimbun, articles 1941/ 44

Senshi Sosho Vol. 96 *Nanto Homen Kaigun Sakusen*

Gatto Tesshu Go, Southeastern Area Naval Operations

Kodochosho (operational logs in *kanji/katakana*)

The following *kokutai* (hand-written *kanji*): Misawa, 1, 2, 752, 582, Chitose, 703, 4, 14, 802, 31, 204, 253, 151, 251, 501, 552, Takao, Mihoro, Genzan, Tainan, Kisarazu, Toko, 851, 702, Yokohama, Kanoya, 751, and other records for 11th Air Fleet and 4th Air Fleet.

Crashed Enemy Aircraft and other Intelligence Reports (CEAR)

Japanese Aircraft Plates and Markings Report No. 68 "Life of Japanese Combat Airplanes," 20 March 1945

CEAR Type 99 Carrier Dive Bomber Model 22, crashed late July 1943 on Baanga Island west of New Georgia

CEAR Number 12, 10 December 1943.

CEAR pertaining to crash of 10 September 1942, off NW Coast of New Georgia, Solomons.

CEAR No. 48, "Information Based on Translations of Name Plates and Stencils from BETTY - Serial Number 1365

AWM54 Item 423/4/92, Intelligence Reports of Japanese Aircraft.

Documents from Betty T-359, Koolpinyah Station, Northern Territory on 23 November 1942 (including test flight logs).

Reproductions and translations of 44 nameplates and painted markings held by AWM.

Miscellaneous

Airpower Magazine Volume 24, No. 4 July 1994 "Spying Behind Japanese Lines with the Coastwatchers in the South Pacific" by Michael Freeman

Air'Tell Research Report "D3A1 Serial Numbers" by Jim Long

Pacificwrecks.com and website owner Justin Taylan

j-aircraft.com (numerous entries)

Nagaishi Masataka Kaigun Kokutai Nenshi, Tokyo January 1961 (sampled lightly as document is incomplete).

HQ 1st Marine Division, periodic report on enemy activity Solomons islands, less Guadalcanal 30 Sept 1942 (including captured airmen).

Chitose Ku Claudes at Rabaul in early February 1942. All tail codes have been removed by the wartime censor.

INDEX OF NAMES